D0906625

New Patterns of Work

New Patterns of Work

Edited by
David Clutterbuck

ST. MARTIN'S PRESS New York

© Gower Publishing Company Limited 1985
Chapter 4 © McGraw-Hill International Publications Company Ltd

All rights reserved. For information, write:
St. Martin's Press, Inc., 175 Fifth Avenue, New York, NY 10010
Printed in Great Britain
First published in the United States of America in 1985

Library of Congress Cataloging in Publication Data

Main entry under title:
New patterns of work.
Includes index.
1. Work – Addresses, essays, lectures. 2. Work
environment – Addresses, essays, lectures.
I. Clutterbuck, David.

HD4901 . N48   1985   306′ . 36   85-1960

ISBN 0–312–56842–8

Contents

Notes on Contributors

JOHN ATKINSON
Research fellow at the Institute of Manpower Studies, he studied economics at Oxford University and industrial relations at Warwick University. He then acted as a research officer for several trade unions. At IMS he is responsible for the Institute's employment policy research programme.

SVEN G. ATTERHED
Sven G. Atterhed has worked with Lennart Boksjö and Gustaf Delin since 1974, and they formed the Foresight Group, known in Scandinavia for its work with leading companies in new product development and strategic action, in 1979. Together they have created a bold new concept and programme in Sweden to stimulate and systematically pursue entrepreneurial activity by established corporations. The new concept is called '*Intra*preneurship', a word coined first by Gifford Pinchat III, Newhaven, Connecticut, USA. A school has been established since 1979, and has been licensed to the largest management consulting firms in Sweden and in Finland. Members of corporations are trained on how to become successful entrepreneurs *within* the parameters of their current employment. Following this, the Foresight Group established the Foresight Institute in Washington, DC, to test and develop the concept for the US market.

DR DENNIS BUMSTEAD
Managing director of management consultants Fordwell Ltd. He gained a BA in economics at Cambridge, and a PhD in management and organisational psychology from MIT.

He has taught at MIT, Manchester Business School and London Business School and has been a full-time consultant since 1977.

DAVID CLUTTERBUCK

Management journalist and author. Former managing editor of *International Management*, he now writes for *The Times*, the *Observer*, the *Economist*, *Chief Executive*, *Management Today* and other business publications. He is the author or co-author of a number of business books, including *How to be a good corporate citizen* (1981), *The Remaking of Work* (1981) and *The Winning Streak* (1984). He is currently editor of *Issues* and *Sound Business* and a director of several specialised publishing firms, including Independent Training & Educational Media Publishers Ltd (ITEM).

CONTROL DATA CORPORATION

A multinational company, specialising in computers and data services. It has extensive engineering, professional and educational resources which it uses to apply the problem solving abilities of computing to commerce, industry, science and social welfare. Control Data is one of the pioneers of telecommuting.

DR MICHAEL CROSS

Senior fellow at the Technical Change Centre, a research consultant for the Manpower Services Commission and Durham University, and adviser on redundancy and employment change issues. His previous books are *New firm formation and regional development*, *US corporate personnel reduction policies*, *Managing workforce reduction: an international survey* and *Towards the flexible craftsman*.

DR JOHN ECKBLAD

President of the Life Business Development Corporation. He received his Ph.D in business from Case Western Reserve University. He has 15 years' experience as a management consultant to major companies in Europe and the United States, and currently lives in North Carolina.

DR RONNIE LESSEM
Director of New Work Ventures and lecturer on Entrepreneur Management at City University Business School in London. He has a PhD in business development and has spent 6 years helping over 1,000 people set up businesses. He has also worked in several major companies to help create or develop intrapreneurial and innovative ventures.

STEPHEN MAY
He graduated in law from Christ Church, Oxford and has worked for the John Lewis Partnership throughout his career. He has been Director of Personnel since 1978 and was previously Managing Director of Peter Jones.

PROFESSOR PEDRO NUENO
Holding the degree of Doctor of Business Administration from Harvard University, he teaches management at IESE, the business school of the University of Navarra, located in Barcelona, Spain. Professor Nueno has done research and consulting work on industrial management and management of technology. As an adviser to government agencies, he has recently followed up several turnaround projects implemented with government help.

DR BERNHARD TERIET
Professor of Labour Economics at Augsburg University in West Germany, he is well-known in that country as a campaigner for new working patterns.

PAM WALTON
For the last three years Pam Walton has been employed by New Ways To Work, a voluntary organisation currently promoting job sharing. She is one of four workers sharing two full-time posts. Before this she worked for the Equal Opportunities Commission, carrying out research into job sharing, including the first survey of job sharers in this country, published by the EOC in 1981. For the previous seven years she worked as a town planner, and tried unsuccessfully to share her planning job in 1977.

Introduction

David Clutterbuck

In any predictive work the farther one departs from present trends, the closer the conclusions come to crystal ball gazing. For this reason, all the contributions in this anthology are concerned with what is already happening, or observable trends that can be expected to gain in momentum. Even though many of these trends are still largely embryonic, they are likely to grow to become accepted and commonplace options in both working careers and work organisation.

Each of the phenomena described in the following pages is a response to external change – political, social, economic and technological. The pace of change (especially in technology, where a major worry for many companies at the leading edge is how to recoup investment in new products before the next technological advance makes them obsolete) is forcing organisations to become much more flexible in their response to external change agents. That, in turn, obliges them to be more flexible in their internal organisation, including the way in which they organise people. A whole new vocabulary is beginning to grow up around this sea-change, with terms such as flexible manufacturing and flexible manning now coming into common use.

In effect, everything about the working environment is currently in the melting pot, including:

1 How we work,
2 Where we work,
3 When we work,
4 Why we work, and
5 How we are compensated for work.

HOW WE WORK

Technology is rapidly changing all types of work. On the shop floor, robotics (still not widely applied in British companies) are beginning to take over dangerous, repetitive and labour-intensive work. The fully automated factory, though still limited in the scope of its operations, is already a reality in Japan. The flexible manufacturing systems of the late 1980s will gradually allow companies to establish much closer links between the market and their production capabilities. Instead of being production-dominated, with production economies dictating what was most profitable to sell because of the need for long production runs, the enterprise with flexible manufacturing can now fit products exactly to market needs as they change.

In the office, traditional routines are being recast by the new communications technologies, which make corporate information available to anyone with the correct access code. One, as yet largely unrealised, implication of this is that classical business hierarchies can be overturned. Secretaries, for example, suddenly have the opportunity to expand their role at the expense of the middle manager. According to temp agency Manpower, tomorrow's secretaries will be much more highly skilled than their current counterparts. They will possess the ability to collate and summarise complex information from a number of sources, and, with their keyboard and presentation skills, they will pose a formidable challenge to the manager.

At all levels and functions in the company further radical change is likely as a result of the introduction of expert systems – computers that can within a limited area of expertise store the knowledge of the most proficient people in a particular field and apply it to new problems. On the production floor, inspection by expert systems will not need to be given an exhaustive list of faults to look for. Instead it will deduce that something is wrong and reject the faulty product accordingly. The production staff, too, will find expert systems acting as the interface between their often very basic knowledge of how equipment works and complex computer-controlled operating systems that may be beyond their understanding.

In the offices and in the professions expert systems will be used as 'second opinions' to which employees and managers can refer to check their own judgement. This means, in effect, that people can be trusted with greater authority at the lower levels, because the likelihood of their making serious blunders is reduced. It does not mean that the computer can be trusted to make the decisions on their behalf (although expert systems may be right in their answers more often than all but the most expert human experts, they become wildly inaccurate when faced with questions outside their defined area of expertise). But it does impose a discipline in that, to reject the computer's diagnosis – which comes with an analysis of the logic that led to the conclusion – the employee must come up with adequate reasons.

Expert systems will also be extensively used in training. Instead of learning from a mentor or in a classroom, employees will absorb thinking processes by working closely with the expert system.

Social pressures are also influencing the *how* of work. The rise in the level of education within our society has produced generations of workers who expect to be consulted about the content of their jobs and to be given increased freedom in how they go about achieving their task objectives. This fortunately fits in with the growing recognition among employers that participation leads to commitment, which in turn results in higher productivity and improved quality of product or services.

One of the issues to be faced in the future is that badly designed computer systems may negate these positive moves by imposing excessively rigid routines. For this reason, the relating of the communications aspects of each job to the new technologies available will be an increasing preoccupation for top management. Research from the United States and West Germany indicates that new technology applied against the grain in communications terms may actually decrease productivity. To apply rigid computer systems to a job where the decision-making processes tend to be unstructured or unique to each case, for example, will work against efficiency.

WHERE WE WORK

Whereas most people used to expect to work for a large company or for a nationalised industry or a government department, now the pendulum is in full swing back towards the small business sector. The diminution of Civil Service numbers is a political phenomenon, potentially reversible; but the collapse of the large company employment market is a more significant trend, born out of economic change, notably the maturing of big company industrial sectors and the need to compete internationally by holding down labour costs.

Increasingly, the numbers of jobs are being made up by small firms. At the same time, cottage industry, once virtually written off as a source of employment, is making a come-back, through one-man businesses and telecommuting (working at home, connected to the office by a computer and telephone line).

WHEN WE WORK

Economic pressures and social awareness have brought increasing numbers of women into the workforce, many of them working part-time. Between March 1983 and March 1984 an additional 263,000 jobs were created in the UK. No fewer than 213,000 of these jobs were part-time, for women. Full-time jobs for men rose by only 6,000. Over the past 12 years some 2.3 million full-time jobs have been lost from the labour force, while an additional 1.3 million part-time jobs have been created. The UK is already one of the countries with the highest proportion of part-time workers in Europe, and the trend can be expected to continue at least for the rest of this decade.

However, the distinction between part- and full-time work

is becoming increasingly blurred with 'full-time' meaning anything from 32 to 40 hours a week (plus) according to occupation. Working hours can be expected to continue their century-long decline well into the 1990s. The 40-hour engineering industry week has finally (after a lengthy strike) been breached in West Germany and had already been cut to 39 hours in England in 1981. In 1955 the West German working week was 49.8 hours, so that it has fallen more than 20 per cent in just under 30 years. There seems every reason to expect the trend to continue.

But weekly hours are only one form of working time reduction – equally important are holidays, sabbaticals, and early retirement. When considering the total annual hours, British full-time employees worked an average of 1,833 versus 1,773 for West Germans, 1,904 for Americans and 2,101 for the Japanese. The pressures to reduce working times are primarily social, but their roots lie partially in technological and economic changes that make some form of work-sharing both feasible and desirable.

A more flexible approach to working time requires consideration of new concepts such as job sharing (where two people take on the responsibilities of a single job between them) and flexible working years. In both cases there are significant benefits to both employee and employer. The employer gains not merely flexibility but increased productivity.

Equally important is the changing nature of shift work. Here again searches are being made for flexible new approaches that will bridge the gap between people's growing reluctance to work shifts and the increasing demand for shiftwork in both process and service industries. In Belgium, Philips has experimented with shift patterns at its factory at Roulers, West Flanders, where it now has two sets of workers. One set works a normal 38-hour, five-day week; the other works two 12-hour weekend shifts and is paid as if it worked 36 hours. This has created about fifteen extra jobs, but these were covered by the additional and more flexible use of equipment. Again, the impetus is part social, part economic.

WHY WE WORK

Working people are rapidly dividing into two categories – those who see their job solely as a means to obtain money and those who see it as a means to personal fulfilment. The concept of work as a good thing in itself, regardless of what it accomplishes (the fear of idle hands getting up to mischief), no longer holds sway. Once they have satisfied the basic financial needs, most people either work to finance other interests, such as fishing, hang-gliding, gardening or the home, or else they work because they enjoy what they are doing and feel caught up in its purpose. For this reason, many people on both sides of the employment market are espousing what some white-collar union leaders refer to as the 'usefulness ethic' – the concept that while traditional paid employment may not be available to or wanted by all, the ability and opportunity to perform a useful task in society should and must be available. This brings into the fore the question of compensation.

HOW WE ARE COMPENSATED FOR WORK

Several issues are relevant here. They include greater equality in pay for disadvantaged groups (a social pressure), competitive wage pricing (an economic and political issue), and the nature of the way payment is calculated (an economic issue).

The pressure for equal opportunities is increasingly being focused on issues of pay, particularly with regard to the largest 'minority' – women. In the US, business associations are fighting a rearguard action against feminist organisa- tions' attempts to raise women's wages to men's levels by comparison of 'job ghettos' (job categories predominantly occupied by women and hence lower paid) with male- dominated occupations. The causes of the disparities are complex, not least because of the high proportion of women who take time out of their careers for child-rearing, and exact comparisons are very difficult to make. But the pressure for roughly equal pay for similar grades of work across the sexual lines will grow and may well modify the laws of supply and demand, especially as more and more women assess their market value above what the market is prepared to pay. We may also expect to see heightened activity by women's groups within trade unions, with special focus on issues of pay.

Never strongly entrenched in the UK in the first place other than in engineering, transport and the state-owned enterprises, nation-wide pay bargaining across Europe is becoming less and less tenable with the widening of the gap between those companies that can afford to pay and those that cannot. Even in West Germany, a bastion of nation-wide bargaining, recent agreements set a base above which each company's employees bargain for what they can get. Pay flexibility is increasingly the norm.

The extremes to which this could go are illustrated by the experience of General Motors' Packard plant at Warren, Ohio. Agreements for temporary wage cuts in times of special crisis have become quite commonplace in the United States, and have been known in Britain too. But Packard has gone much farther in the size and permanency of the cuts it has made.

The plant's main problem was that its wage costs, at $19.60 an hour in salary and benefits, were too high in comparison with independent suppliers ($6 an hour) or employees in Mexico ($1 an hour). As an alternative to making 2,700 of the nearly 9,000 employees redundant, GM offered a revolutionary deal, which effectively created a two-tier wage structure. All present employees continued to draw their current level of pay and received guarantees of job security, but agreed not to hinder the natural attrition of manpower. All new employees start at $6 an hour, but are able to join the ranks of the established employees as core workers retire or leave for other reasons. This experiment is being watched with great interest by other US companies and could form a pattern for employment in mature industries.

The other critical issue is the contractual relationship between employer and employee. Several of the chapters that follow explore the loosening of the bonds between the two sides of the labour contract and the gradual move towards a subcontractual role for many current employees. As this becomes more pronounced, companies will be obliged to look at the degree of flexibility in which they use and motivate those people who remain in traditional employment. While the need to assess and compensate some jobs on a time basis will continue (a nightwatchman may be paid just for being there, for example), it will make much more sense in most cases to tie pay partially or wholly to results where these can fairly be said to rest in the employee's hands. In some cases it may be necessary to redesign jobs so that people do have responsibility for measurable output, whether it be in quantity of product, achievement of a level of service, or some other form. In effect, all elements in the production chain – from supplier through internal labour to distributor – will, for the first time since the Industrial Revolution, operate on similar contractual arrangements.

These are just a few of the important changes taking place now in working patterns. As the external changes accelerate, we can expect to see a constant flow of ideas and experiments in this area. Some, like the 4-day week, will blossom and fade because the time is not yet ripe; others will take root swiftly and deeply, affecting the working lives of millions. What all these innovations represent together is a realisation that work and our approach to it will be subject to frequent change, and that flexibility in behaviour patterns by both employers and the people whose time and services they hire is an essential requirement of tomorrow at work.

1 The brave new world of work

David Clutterbuck

This chapter and those that immediately follow are concerned with change in the corporate organisation and the implications of such change for working patterns.

As little as 20 years ago, had anyone in a major company thought to ask 'What are we in business for?', the answer would in most cases have been 'To make a profit'. Now many companies set themselves additional corporate objectives that cover their perceived obligations to a much wider range of stakeholders than their shareholders and the banks.

In re-examining their objectives and how they will achieve them, these companies frequently find themselves putting the clock back to ideas and behaviours abandoned as outmoded but now enjoying a renaissance. For example, job security, originally a privilege for the faithful retainer or long-serving employee but swept away with apparent finality during the recent recession, now seems to be making a come-back, particularly in the United States. An article in the *Harvard Business Review* (Nov.–Dec. 1983) by James F. Bolt examines why this is happening and finds several reasons, including the following:

1 The cost of laying people off – one large US manufacturer spent $50 million in severance pay and benefits in 1982 (still a fleabite by comparison with the pay-outs by some European nationalised industries).
2 The operational disadvantages – the damage to morale, public reputation and the instability caused to the working environment.

3 The increasing pressure for job security against the background of lower annual growth rates in the number of jobs while numbers entering the job market increase.

4 The difficulty of installing and implementing productivity programmes without full co-operation of the employees, something that cannot be given if they fear greater productivity will mean the loss of their jobs. US companies have absorbed this lesson particularly from Japan, where, in large companies and for the core group of workers, although not for women nor for the vast army of employees seconded from suppliers, job security and active willing participation in productivity improvement go hand in hand.

Bolt points to a study by *Chemical and Engineering News* in the late 1960s that examined the differences between high technology companies that had suffered heavy lay-offs and those that had not. The only major difference was that the second group had proceeded to 'establish a policy not to have lay-offs, and institute good management to carry out that policy'.

Interestingly, some years ago Sir Hector Laing offered a 'contract' to United Biscuits' employees guaranteeing employment security or income protection for 5 years after 5 years' service and up to retirement after 10 years' service if the employees would agree to allocate 20 per cent of added value to reinvestment as the first charge and to work that investment efficiently and flexibly. This offer was not accepted for a number of complex reasons. In the last few years attitudes to security of employment have changed significantly, and the idea is still being discussed under the name of the wage–work bargain.

Such moves, however, only serve to focus top management attention on what groups and classifications of employees are essential and to limit regular employment with all its privileges to those groups. This is discussed in greater detail by John Atkinson and Michael Cross in Chapters 2 and 3 respectively. Suffice to say that a clearer yet broader focusing of objectives is encouraging rather than stemming the pace of change in corporate organisation. The principal elements of that change process are:

1 A gradual contraction of the number of employees in large companies and a shrinkage of the number of hierarchical levels.
2 The break-up of large companies into federations of semi-independent small profit centres.
3 A corresponding growth in the independent small business sector.
4 New relations between small and large business.

Out of these changes will come both new employment practices and new career patterns.

THE CONTRACTION OF BIG COMPANY EMPLOYMENT

There is scarcely a major employer in the UK that has not made substantial reductions in employee numbers in the past 5 years. It is easy to put this shake-out down to the effects of the recession and to assume that numbers will climb again as the economy returns to boom. That assumption is not borne out by the intentions of the companies, however, who have no intention of increasing their numbers and in many cases intend to continue reducing them. What is happening is that increases in productivity, in both white and blue collar employment, are soaking up almost all new job opportunities as they arise.

ICI, for example, averaged 84,000 employees in 1979. By 1984 it had only 61,000 and is unlikely to increase numbers again. Blue Circle's cement interests, with 12,000 employees in 1979 and 9,000 in 1984, show no signs of reversal of the downward trend in employee numbers. Cadbury's cut its workforce from 10,000 to 7,000 over the same period, mainly due to increased production efficiencies. The number of employees in Plessey decreased from 53,000 in 1980 to 39,000 in 1984.

The tale is the same in almost every manufacturing

industry, including electronics, where assembly work is now rapidly being taken over by automation. Service industries are not immune; British Airways reduced its workforce from 58,000 in 1979 to 37,000 in 1984. Yet employment decreases in the service industries are often masked because of changing employment strategy. Abbey National Building Society is one such company which superficially appears to have increased its employment, from 7,200 in 1979 to 8,100 in 1984. However, since 1974 full-time staff have been reduced while part-time staff have doubled, and this last group does not include the 470 casual workers who are currently employed. The building society is now concentrating on creating a decentralised organisation with small-staffed autonomous units. Consequently, a comparison of the numbers of full-time staff employed since 1979 with the number of new branches established shows clearly that the average numbers of employees have in fact decreased.

These job losses have hit all levels of the corporate hierarchy, but one group particularly hard hit has been middle management, which has been sliced by up to 50 per cent in some industries in certain countries. An estimate in *International Management* puts the decline at about 15 per cent of middle management positions globally between 1979 and 1982. Again these jobs are generally not being replaced. The reasons behind this phenomenon are several:

1 General restructuring of company organisations leaves fewer slots for middle managers.
2 Many companies are trying to increase the span of control of their managers, to prevent them being locked into narrow-focused jobs. Ford, which in 1982 had already increased the span of control of its middle managers from three people to five (cutting their numbers by 10 per cent in the process), has its eyes on an eventual ratio of one to seven.
3 There is a general agreement now that middle management ranks were heavily swollen in most large companies and that the consequent bureaucracy worked against efficiency.
4 Large companies often accumulate a 'layer of clay' – a

stratum of middle management with little real function that preoccupies itself by interpreting instructions from above and filtering information from below. As a result, the bottom of the organisation has little clear idea of top management thinking and top management has little idea of what is happening on the shop floor. Removing that layer of clay allows information to flow more freely – something most companies now recognise as an essential part of maintaining their competitive edge.

5 New technology can and does do most of the information-processing and exception-reporting that used to be middle management's province.

The cutting out of middle management positions automatically means smaller hierarchies and that fits well with the flexible organisation to which so many large companies are trying to move. The efficient modern large company (with a few significant exceptions such as retail) has a small headquarters and a large number of operating units. In most cases it will have several fewer layers of management than a decade ago. This trend will continue as the need for swift action demands easier and faster communication between the top strategic level and the bottom operational levels.

The main implication of this trend is that large companies no longer offer the career opportunities they used to. While a small core group of employees may enjoy permanent secure employment, they will be in the minority. Moreover, the number of openings at middle and senior management levels will continue to shrink, raising the problem of how to motivate good employees when the promotion prospects are small.

THE BREAK-UP OF LARGE COMPANIES INTO SMALL SEMI-INDEPENDENT UNITS

Part of this growing flexibility is a strong tide towards splitting large companies into multiple small profit centres. Although it has been fashionable over the decades to oscillate between centralisation and decentralisation, the trend now appears to be much more fundamental than a mere swing of fashion. What is now happening in the private sector (and might perhaps, with a lot of imagination, occur in the public sector in due course, with enough political will) is the general collapse of bureaucracy.

What makes a company split in this way? For Plessey, it was a matter of the need to compete more effectively. Over a decade, it broke up its centralised bureaucracy and appointed those managers capable of taking on profit centre responsibility to run their own empires. The result has been a revitalisation of the company, with unit managers now becoming specialists in their own area and able to sell with confidence against international competition. For Street shoemaker Clark's, the lesson emerged during the Second World War, when the main factory was taken over for munitions work. Forced to work in lots of small units, the company found that productivity rocketed.

Racal, the fastest growing British electronics company, adopts a similar approach, spawning new companies for each new batch of products and attempting to keep the numbers of people in a single profit centre down to 500 or less. The benefits come in speed of response – the managing director of the unit does not need to ask anyone else's permission when a swift market decision is needed – and in the personalised and committed atmosphere that can be created in operations of this size.

Organisational division opens up opportunities for employees to gain general management experience at a much lower level and much earlier than would normally be the case in the traditional organisational pyramid. It also allows for a considerable degree of experimentation, since what happens in one unit does not necessarily create a precedent for others. In particular, it makes it possible to cultivate intrapreneurs (see Chapter 6).

THE RISE OF THE SMALL BUSINESS SECTOR

To a certain extent, small companies have been taking up

the slack created in the employment market by the shake-outs in the major companies – at least in the United States, Britain and Eire. According to the Department of Employment figures for 1971 to 1981, small firms provide 31 per cent of all new jobs, although they have only 13 per cent by value of the total sales.

Exactly what is behind the boom in small business is difficult to establish. In the UK the climate and encouragement given by successive Conservative governments has probably played a significant part, but it is by no means certain that growth in the small business sector would not have taken place under a different administration. There seems to be emerging, both in the US and the UK, a new attitude of entrepreneurship. This stems partially from a realisation that working for a large firm is in most cases no longer the lifetime option it used to be, and that there may be greater stability of employment in taking one's destiny into one's own hands. It also stems from a growing disparity between skills availability and demand. In spite of high unemployment, certain skills are in short supply, especially at the top end of the ability scale. Because more and more companies are prepared to pay extra for quality in the labour they hire, the really good employee in any occupation can generally make more on the open market than as a traditional employee. This trend is likely to be an established feature of the next two decades and perhaps beyond.

The new small businesses are almost all in the service industries. One reason is that selling acquired skills is usually a service function, although it may sometimes involve specialised manufacturing. Another reason is that the start-up cost of investment in capital equipment for manufacturing is relatively high for the individual with little or no personal capital. This situation may change as automation reduces some equipment costs. Few small businesses could have afforded their own computer or word processor a decade ago, for example. Now few cannot afford one.

The cost of business start-up has been reduced not only by the various grant and loan guarantee schemes, but also by the rise of new forms of start-ups. Franchising, for example, is now a major growth area, with the numbers of franchise operations doubling between 1979 and 1984, and the annual sales of the members of the British Franchise Association growing at 16 per cent per annum. The US (not actually the home of the idea, but certainly the place where it has been exploited most fully) has more than 250,000 franchise businesses. The method allows the entrepreneur to draw on the experience of someone who has already been through all the problems of setting up such a business and provides him with a national name and advertising programme that would otherwise be far beyond his means.

Buy-outs, too, are becoming increasingly common as large companies focus on their core businesses and shake out those that are not an easy fit or take up excessive top management time. In 1977 there were only thirteen management buy-outs in Britain. In 1983, there were 170, ranging in size from a few tens of thousands of pounds to over £50 million.

The number of small firms (those of under 100 employees) is also rapidly increasing, and these will gradually play a more important role in the economy in the future. Indeed, out of the 2 million firms now existing, 700,000 are small firms, and on average 150,000 small firms are born every year.

One of the more interesting phenomena is the stirrings of a movement for more women to become independent entrepreneurs. To some extent this is due to the increasing confidence women have in their working ability, yet this trend is also fuelled by the twin pressures of more and more women seeking satisfying work while traditional women's jobs are replaced by technology. Studies of female entrepreneurs indicate significant differences in their background and motivations. In particular, they are four times more likely than men to have had a parent in business on his or her own account, and many of them start businesses much closer to retirement than is usual with men.

NEW RELATIONS BETWEEN LARGE AND SMALL BUSINESS

These changes are starting to affect the way big business and small businesses deal with each other. By decentralising, large companies are attempting to create many of the attitudes and capabilities of small companies, and this inevitably makes them more aware of small company problems.

The moves by many of the largest companies in the country to encourage new small businesses, for example, through more enlightened payment policies and the rash of enterprise trusts are an evidence of that new relation. Shell, for example, goes so far as to invite local small companies into its operations to show them the kind of goods and services it needs and how to go about obtaining part of that business.

The motivation of these companies is only partially altruistic. They recognise that small businesses and the people they employ are tomorrow's customers.

As a result, large companies are increasingly willing to contemplate new ways of working *with* small companies. They are looking for mutual benefits – holding down the numbers of core employees, while creating relations that go beyond the traditional supplier/purchaser model. Among the concepts being experimented with are:

1 Taking up slack in their distribution or export functions by making the services available to smaller companies with whom they already have an association.
2 Exchanging staff between the large and small companies to transfer know-how (a common practice in Japan).
3 Encouraging managers to develop new ideas as independent ventures, in which the large company retains a minority interest (both STC and ICI have expressed interest in this area and at least one French company has carried out experiments).
4 Taking a small investment stake in promising small companies, to help them finance mutually supportive new product development. For example, Ramtek Corporation

in the United States put $2 million into a tiny company, Digital Productions Inc., according to *Business Week* (25 June 1984) to develop the software for a powerful imaging system the big company felt it needed to balance its product range. Says *Business Week*, 'In the past, big companies typically bought up little ones when they wanted their expertise. But in many cases, the acquiring corporations mismanaged their new property and lost the very people and creative environment that attracted them in the first place'.

By giving up any idea of *controlling* the small company, the large company retains the best of all worlds. It has working for it in a close but not stifling relation key people who probably would not consider working for it as traditional employees. In addition, it avoids all the problems of spending top management time supervising minor outposts of the corporate empire. This pattern is becoming increasingly common in high technology and in leading edge service companies.

5 Linked subcontracting (described in Chapter 4) is a further example of this refashioning of relations between large companies and small suppliers. Not long ago such experiments would have been dismissed as causing too much trouble and disruption. Now they are seen as the pattern for the future, as essential ingredients in the recipe for flexibility in the modern corporation.

NEW EMPLOYMENT PRACTICES AND CAREER PATTERNS

It follows from these various trends that more and more people – indeed, the majority – will before long be working in small rather than large companies. That poses problems of transition (people used to working for 20 years or more in a large company where resources are readily available may find the transition to small company life traumatic) and of in-company training, because small companies do not normally have the time or resources for comprehensive training programmes and have been used to parasiting trained staff from their larger brethren. We can expect to see a growth in collaborative training schemes, either between a large company and a number of smaller, independent customers and suppliers, or between groups of similar small companies. In the former case it represents an opportunity for the large company to spread the costs of its training department and move it some way towards being a profit centre.

Another consequence, hastened by the speeding up of the rate of natural obsolescence of many jobs, is a break-down of the traditional one career, one employer approach. As the recent fierce arguments over portable pensions has revealed, only a small proportion of people remain with one employer their whole working life and the number of registrations annually at job centres points to job turnover on a massive scale. The Manpower Services Commission annually helps place 1.7 million people into new jobs, and in 1983–4 informally dealt with 34 million inquiries about job vacancies. Tomorrow's career pattern is likely to intermingle school–work–retirement in a far more flexible manner, with both men and women alternating between part- and full-time work as domestic circumstances (children, intensive study for further education) demand a constant knowledge renewal to be an important part of retaining one's basic skills and marketability.

Future career patterns will have to be shaped according to new criteria that match the new attitudes emerging. Movement between small and large firms will become much easier, particularly at middle and senior management level, where it is now often difficult because of the uncertainty of the career impact of a period outside the mainstream of big business. Working patterns that are likely to become more common include:

1 *Sabbaticals*, which have been available in Australia since 1951 and are now an established and accepted part of employment practice. The practical minimum requirement for entitlement to a 13-week sabbatical in that country is 15 years' continuous employment with the same employer, but there is pressure to adjust the rules to allow sabbaticals after a reduced number of years with *any*

employer. One of the problems with the current rules is that they penalise women, who have much lower continuity of service.

Some British companies offer sabbaticals, and the topic is gaining increased attention and interest. Chapter 9 examines one company's experience of a sabbatical programme.

2 *Decruitment*, a term invented in Denmark, which allows managers to plan ahead to step down into lower positions in an agreed number of years before retirement. It destroys the myth that a career must continue upwards to be successful; most of those who take decruitment are pleased to have the opportunity to wind down from a peak.

3 *Intrapreneurship*, where employees become entrepreneurs within the company (see Chapter 6).

4 *The multiple job holder*, who develops a number of marketable skills and plies them according to market demand and his own interests. For example, a research chemist may hire his skills alternately as a consultant, a traditional laboratory-based researcher, and as a specialist analyst within a stockbroking firm. A journalist may develop the additional skills of market research and public relations. One college lecturer split his time between his academic work and a part-time post as a practising personnel manager in a City institution. This type of working pattern is becoming increasingly common and provides a valuable resource for companies which do not wish to expand their core employees yet wish to have particular skills on call.

Most of these trends will be examined in greater detail in the chapters that follow.

2 The changing corporation

John Atkinson

In this chapter John Atkinson, Research Fellow at the Institute of Manpower Studies, shows that UK employers are beginning to introduce new employment and manpower strategies which are more appropriate to the uncertain economic and market prospects of the 1980s than many of the orthodox notions about manpower management and internal labour markets which grew up in the 1960s and 1970s.

'British firms don't have manpower strategies; they just have manpower tactics writ large.' This comment, made by a senior personnel director in response to questions about new employment strategies, seems to sum up both the weaknesses and the strengths of British manpower management. On the one hand, it implies that manpower policies are often the unplanned outcome of business initiatives which have been taken without serious consideration of their manpower implications. But on the other hand, it also implies that such policies are subordinate to business needs and do not have any independent rationale. It also suggests that responses to changing economic circumstances are likely to be empirical and pragmatic. A programme of research and advisory work conducted at IMS during 1983–4 has been considering where such empiricism and pragmatism is taking corporate manpower policy in the UK. This chapter outlines some of its main findings, which may be briefly summarised as follows.

Under the combined influences of profound economic recession, uncertainty about market growth, technological change in both products and production methods, and reductions in working time, British employers are beginning to introduce novel and unorthodox formations in their deployment of labour. They mark a significant break with the conventional, unitary and hierarchical internal labour markets which dominate UK manpower management both in theory and in practice. These innovations are intended to secure greater flexibility from the workforce, in terms of its responsiveness both to the level of economic activity (numerical flexibility) and to the nature of that activity (functional flexibility).

In our view such changes are as yet pragmatic and opportunist, rather than driven by a conscious strategy. As a result they are greatly assisted by the current stagnation of the labour market and the resulting industrial relations advantage conferred on most employers. We do not expect such changes to be merely temporary expediences, however, as their perceived advantages to employers are likely to persist beyond the current labour market climate. Because of this, such marginal changes seem to us to be the precursors of a new model for firms' organisation of their labour forces which we can expect to develop more strongly in years to come.

Although there are strong sectoral and company-centred differences in the precise forms favoured, the emerging model is one of horizontal segmentation into a core workforce, which will conduct the organisation's key firm-specific activities, surrounded by a cluster of peripheral groups. Their twin purpose is to protect the core group from numerical employment fluctuations while conducting the host of non-specific and subsidiary activities which all organisations require and generate. The core group is required to be functionally flexible; the numerical flexibility secured from the use of peripheral groups provides the core group with employment security as the basis of their functional flexibility in the face of change. Peripheral groups may be made up of employees or of workers brought in on a subcontract basis. The exploitation of a range of alternative contractual and working-time arrangements permits firms to secure precisely the number and type of such secondary workers that they might require at any time.

There are strong job-related, technical, institutional and labour market influences on the deployment of such un-orthodox manning strategies, but the major influence on the choice is likely to be the chosen business strategy of the organisation. Whatever combination of groups is intro-duced, the impact on employees is likely to be divisive, with the employment security, promotion prospects and condi-tions of employment of core group workers differentiating them markedly from peripherals. As trade union organisa-tion among such peripherals is likely to be undermined, this may itself increase the differentiation. We envisage no necessary incompatibility between management and union aims for core group workers, however.

PRESSURES FOR CHANGE

Although it is possible to identify some sectors of the economy and some firms whose experience has been different, several important common themes can be found underpinning the employment plans of most UK firms. Among the most important are:

1 *Market stagnation.* The combination of world recession, of the UK's unusually deep and prolonged share of that recession, and of a widespread inability to compete effectively in world markets, has led to a managerial imperative with the permanent reduction of unit labour costs.
2 *Job loss.* Virtually all UK firms have undergone an enforced and dramatic reduction in employment levels, which have often been as expensive in cash terms as they have been painful for employee relations.
3 *Uncertainty.* Despite official optimism about a national growth rate of 3 per cent during the middle 1980s, many firms appear privately more cautious about the pace of an upswing, and, more importantly, are not relying on growth being sustained. As a result, such firms are anxious not to overcommit themselves in terms of employment or investment.

4 *Technological change.* The increasing pace and decreasing cost of technological change means that the firm (and its employees in particular) needs to be capable of responding quickly to substantial changes in either product lines or production methods (and probably both).
5 *Working time.* As reductions in basic hours have continued, so employers have increasingly been forced to reconsider the most effective deployment of worked time. This has led to a widespread view among employers that any further reductions of working time can only be sustained through restructuring worked time, often in quite unconventional ways.

As a result, firms have found themselves under pressure to find more flexible ways of manning which take account of these new market realities. They have put a premium on achieving a workforce which can respond quickly, easily and cheaply to unforeseen changes, which may need to contract as smoothly as it expands, in which worked time precisely matches job requirements, and in which unit labour costs can be held down.

At the same time, employers have recognised that the current state of the labour market, with high unemployment, few shortages of labour, and a weakened trade union movement, will help them secure these aims. There are both strong pressures to achieve a more flexible workforce, therefore, and greater opportunities to do so now than in the past.

WHAT KIND OF FLEXIBILITY?

Our research suggests that firms are really looking for three kinds of flexibility – functional, numerical and financial. The first two are sought as operational necessities; the third largely as a means of implementing them.

FUNCTIONAL FLEXIBILITY

Employees can be redeployed quickly and smoothly between activities and tasks under this form of flexibility.

This might mean moving multi-skilled craftsmen between mechanical, electrical and pneumatic jobs; it might mean moving workers between indirect and direct production jobs; or it might mean a complete change of career from, say, draughtsman to technical sales. As products and production methods change, functional flexibility implies that the same labour force changes with them, in both the short and medium term.

NUMERICAL FLEXIBILITY

This form of flexibility allows the headcount to be quickly and easily increased or decreased in line with even short-term changes in the level of demand for labour. It might mean that hire and fire policies can be more easily implemented, or that hiring gives way to a looser contractual relation between manager and worker, or that worked time is organised on a more responsive basis than regular weekly basic hours. The end result would be that at any time the number employed/working exactly matched the number needed.

FINANCIAL FLEXIBILITY

This sort of flexibility is sought for two reasons. First, pay and other employment costs will reflect the state of supply and demand in the external labour market. Of course, there is little novel in the suggestion that employers wish to hire labour as cheaply as possible. The significance lies more in relativities and differentials between groups of worker than in an across-the-board push to reduce wages, and the implications include a continued shift to plant level bargaining and widening differentials between skilled and unskilled worker. Secondly, and probably of greater importance in the long term, pay flexibility means a shift to new pay and remuneration systems that facilitate either numerical or functional flexibility, such as assessment-based pay systems in place of rate-for-the-job systems.

*****

There is little that is new in any of these management
aspirations, but what is new is the growing trend for firms
explicitly to seek all three forms of flexibility consistently
and built-in to their basic approach to manning rather than
an additional extra secured through a productivity deal. So
widespread have these aspirations become that many
employers expect them to restructure the work experience
of most workers.

FLEXIBILITY AND CORPORATE STRUCTURE

For these employers, a change in the organisation of work is
seen as the best way of achieving greater flexibility from the
workforce. As a result, a new employment model that
makes it much easier for them to secure all three kinds of
flexibility is beginning to emerge.

The new model requires the break-up of the orthodox
hierarchical structure of the firm in such a way that radically
different employment policies can be pursued for different
groups of workers. The new divisions are much less likely to
be based on blue- or white-collar distinctions, but rather on
the separation of jobs that are specific to a particular firm
from those demanding only general skills. Such firm-specific
skills might range from production manager to maintenance
occupations, and the non-specific from systems analyst to
driver. Both can be found at all levels in a company.

The result is shown in Figure 2.1, which represents the
organisational structure which many UK firms are trying to
introduce. Under the new structure the labour force is
broken up into increasingly peripheral, and therefore
numerically flexible, groups of workers clustered about a
numerically stable core group which will conduct the
organisations' key firm-specific activities. At the core the
emphasis is on functional flexibility; shifting to the periphery, numerical flexibility becomes more important. As the
market grows, the periphery expands to take up slack; as
growth slows, the periphery contracts. At the core, only
tasks and responsibilities change; the workers here are
insulated from medium-term fluctuations of the market,

The flexible firm

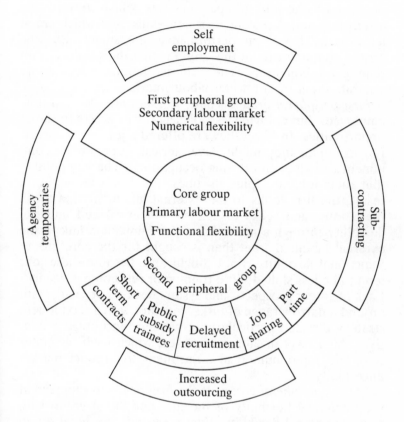

Figure 2.1 Projected organisational structure

whereas those in the periphery are more exposed to them.

Core group. Workers here are full-time permanent career employees, say managers, designers, technical sales staff, quality control staff, technicians and craftsmen. Their employment security is won at the cost of accepting functional flexibility both in the short term (involving cross-trade working, reduced demarcation, and multi-discipline project teams) as well as in the longer term (changing career, retraining etc.). Terms and conditions of employment are designed to promote functional flexibility. This often involves single status conditions, and the displacement of 'rate-for-the-job' by pay systems which reward the acquisition and deployment of new skills, and which are at least partly based on performance assessment. But the central characteristic of this group is that their skills cannot readily be bought-in. The firm is therefore seeking to separate them from a wider labour market.

First peripheral group. These workers are also full-time employees, but enjoying less job security or access to career opportunities. In effect they are offered a job, not a career. For example, they might have clerical, supervisory, component assembly and testing occupations. The key point is that their jobs are 'plug in' ones, not firm-specific. As a result, the firm looks to the external labour market to fill these jobs, and seeks to achieve numerical and financial flexibility through a more direct and immediate link to the external labour market than is sought for the core group. Functional flexibility is not sought and, because these jobs tend to be less skilled, little training or retraining is needed. Lack of career prospects, and systematisation of job content around a narrow range of tasks, together with a recruitment strategy directed particularly at women, encourage a relatively high level of labour turnover, which itself facilitates easy and rapid numerical adjustment to product market uncertainty.

Second peripheral group. If the firm needs to supplement the numerical flexibility of the first peripheral group with some functional flexibility, then a second peripheral group can be distinguished. They are on contracts of employment designed to combine the two. Part-time working is probably the best example of this, the jobs having all the characteristics of those in the first peripheral group, with their deployment often structured to match changing business needs – twilight shifts, overlaid shifts or peak manning etc. Job sharing, short-term contracts, public subsidy trainees and recruitment through temporary contracts all perform a similar function – maximising flexibility while minimising commitment to the worker, job security and career development.

External groups. Where jobs are not at all firm-specific –

because, for example, they are very specialised (e.g. systems analysis) or very mundane (e.g. office cleaning) – firms are increasingly likely to resource them outside, through the use of subcontracting, self-employed jobbers, temporary help agencies etc. This not only permits great numerical flexibility (the firm deciding precisely how much of a particular service it may need at any time), but it also encourages greater functional flexibility than direct employment (as a result of the greater commitment of the self-employed to getting the job done, the greater specialisation of subcontractors, or the relative powerlessness of the worker in this context, according to your taste). Privatisation in public sector agencies is perhaps the best known aspect of this trend to the use of outsourcing, just as the development of networking and teleworking is perhaps the most radical break with past practices. However, both are only part of a much broader externalisation of functions across the broad areas of the UK labour market.

TRAINING GROUPS

Within each of the groups identified above there is a requirement for training. Among core group workers a substantial proportion are likely to be engaged in training and retraining at any one time, in order for their functional flexibility to be achieved. Among peripheral and external groups the rationale for training is somewhat different and unlikely to be given such high priority by the firm itself. As a result, we would expect such training to rely more heavily on public or individual rather than corporate initiative. This may concur with the organisation of the internal labour market along concentric lines, however: for example, trainees sponsored under YTS or the Adult Training Strategy may form one segment of the peripheral group – training within the firm yet not fully part of it, they need not be placed until the completion of training. Clearly the firm's main training interest is unlikely to extend much beyond the core group, and this can lead to training deficiencies, particularly among the external groups.

EXAMPLES OF ORGANISATION

Not all firms are seeking to develop exactly this sort of model, of course. Rather than systematically moving in this direction, many firms are simply taking advantage of a depressed labour market and implementing some aspects of the model as opportunities arise, without any long-term strategy. At the same time, differences between sectors are leading to big differences in the balance between the four groups which firms are seeking. For example, in the construction industry, with the growth of management contracting, the emerging model is for a very small core group allied to a wholly external labour force made up of self-employed and other subcontractors; in the electronic engineering sector, by contrast, all four groups are clearly developing. In the financial services sector there are no external groups, but the emerging pattern is based on a static core, a small and fairly stable first peripheral group and considerable growth of part-time employment in the second peripheral group. The pattern is very much the same in retail distribution and in many of the personal service industries.

Some examples of these changes in work organisation in practice might perhaps make the components of the model clearer, while at the same time illustrating the ways in which such changes are being implemented. The three examples described here clearly show how the general principles outlined in the model are applied in quite different ways to suit the precise needs of the firms in question.

Company A was a medium-sized engineering firm specialising in the design, manufacture and commissioning of plant for the food-processing industry. So volatile was the product market, and so substantial each individual contract, that the firm found itself unable to sustain capacity which it could not fully and continually utilise. In 1980 it began to reorganise its activities on a new basis. First, it withdrew entirely from manufacturing components, laying off over half its manual labour force and building up a network of reliable component suppliers. The next stage was to withdraw gradually from assembly and sub-assembly activities by buying-in more sophisticated and semi-finished products from the network of suppliers. The craftsmen who were displaced by this process were retrained either as technicians in the design function or as installation/maintenance engineers. Those who did not seek, or were not capable of, such retraining were offered early retirement or voluntary redundancy.

The company now consists of a specialist design team and an installation/commissioning/maintenance function. In order to utilise the remaining capacity, the design team has expanded into contract design work for other process plant manufacturers, and the engineering function is beginning to build up a contract maintenance business, both for customers and other local firms. In terms of the model, a functionally flexible core group plus a number of external contract suppliers have supplanted the orthodox employment structure. In this respect Company A looks like much of the UK construction industry.

Company B is a manufacturing arm of a foreign multinational in the electrical and electronic engineering sector. The company was very badly hit by the combination of recession and technological change in the product market and engaged in a severance exercise to cut manning in most functions to that level regarded as sustainable in the long term and enforced by rigid headcount control by the parent. In some activities (maintenance, finance, design, sales) redundant employees were encouraged to set themselves up on a self-employed basis with the company undertaking to contract a minimum level of business with them in their first year. This provided one source of numerical flexibility. Secondly, the company negotiated an agreement with the trade unions which allowed the company to increase output by 15 per cent without recourse to hiring labour. This was to be achieved by greater functional flexibility on the part of employees, supplemented by the use of temporary, agency and self-employed workers brought in as required. Where recruitment to the core was necessary, this would be done initially on the basis of temporary contracts. In terms of the model, considerable numerical flexibility had been achieved, around a stable core group, largely through the creation or expansion of external and peripheral groups of workers.

Company C is a large UK firm in the financial services

sector. Here technological change rather than market instability has been the source of reorganisation. Computerisation has produced a situation where activities which once required many years of training and work experience can now be subject to systematic rules and principles, and as a result can be adequately performed by clerical workers rather than by professionals – one example being the displacement of many underwriting and sales skills which had traditionally formed two of the main career streams in the company. On the sales side the employment of a highly skilled salesforce has been at least partly displaced through the greater use of self-employed, commission-only salesmen and brokers. Among the underwriters the increasing sophistication of the software in use has increasingly meant their displacement by part-time female clerical employees with general keyboard skills and much less extensive firm-specific training. In terms of the model, core group professionals are gradually being displaced by peripheral and external groups. The pattern is a fairly common one throughout much of the financial services sector.

IMPLEMENTING FLEXIBILITY

The extent to which firms are able to implement changes to their employment strategies, and the precise combinations of such innovations, are severely constrained in the short term. Probably the most important constraint is a strong preference for gradualism, particularly where no opportunities for 'a fresh start', such as the opening of new plants, can readily be exploited. The corollary of this is that such changes cannot readily be undone – therefore managers need to have some confidence about the likely duration of changes, particularly to labour market conditions, before they are prepared to commit themselves.

Two distinct problems confronted the managers with whom we discussed the implementation of such a reorganisation of work. First, there was an evident need to decide which functions and activities would be manned in which way, and second, there was the need to devise appropriate styles of management for each group. We examine these in turn below.

DETERMINANTS OF CHANGE

Few of the firms with which we spoke had been able to establish clear criteria for allocating functions to particular segments. In many of them there appeared to be considerable conflict between a 'suck it and see' school and a 'put everything out to contract' school. Nevertheless certain determinants of, and constraints on, reorganisation can be identified.

Job-centred Factors

Many jobs cannot readily be relegated to peripheral or external status. Those jobs which can easily be relegated appear to have the following characteristics:

1 *Restricted training requirements.* The cost and duration of training places a major constraint on firms' readiness to consider new approaches to manning. Speed of training may be particularly important if the anticipated tenure of peripheral workers is low. Even highly skilled jobs can have low training requirements, provided that educational output is (a) appropriate and (b) exploited. Public training (such as YTS) designed to produce transferable skills may reduce the costs and duration of initial training in the firm, and hence extend the likely constituency of secondary jobs.

2 *Internal jobs.* Firms generally prefer to retain jobs calling for contact with the public, customers, suppliers, associates and outside bodies, within the core group.

3 *Prescribed and defined tasks.* Jobs with little autonomy or cumulative decision-making aspects might be organised in the peripheral group, while those whose tasks cannot readily be systemised, or with cumulative and unpredictable decision-making aspects, are not widely believed to be suitable for secondary status. Job definition is of course an even more necessary aspect of external labour

sources – e.g. the use of self-employed or subcontract employees.

Technical/Production Related Factors

Highly fragmented production processes can often employ peripheral workers in some or all functions. Ancillary functions not related to the main production process are often readily transferable into the periphery: catering, cleaning, portering and security represent some fairly unskilled areas which have been externalised by many UK firms in recent years. Technical design, toolmaking, financial and legal activities represent some more skilled support activities which may also be subcontracted. In recent years there has been a considerable expansion of the scope of temporary-help agencies into such fields to take advantage of employers seeking to man such activities on a secondary basis. The central activities of firms, around which orthodox unitary internal labour markets are designed, are less susceptible to reorganisation on this basis, because of the firm-specific nature of the jobs and the requirement for a committed and motivated workforce in such posts. However, one effect of new technology has been to de-skill some jobs by introducing systematic and rational decision-making rules. This shift of the ground rules may offer further potential for movement from core to periphery.

Institutional Factors

Our research suggests that more important than the technical possibilities for reorganisation is the inertia resulting from employers' caution and their concern about the effects of change on industrial relations. In practice, firms who were more familiar with secondary and external forms of employment were more prepared to explore extensions and additions to these forms of employment structures. But the deadweight of conventional practices should not be underestimated. Among unionised firms, 'custom and practice' as well as collective agreements limit the ability of employers to deploy secondary labour at will.

Supply Side Factors

There are two main constraints here. Not all employees are prepared to accept secondary conditions of employment, and managers often express concern about shortcomings in the quality of such workers.

1 *Quantitative aspects.* Insofar as the supply of secondary workers is predicated on a high level of unemployment, firms in more buoyant, or potentially buoyant, labour markets are concerned about the future supply of such employees. Insofar as it is predicated on changing working preferences (for self-employment, temporary work, part-time work, etc.), or on recruiting from different sources (most often women rather than men, but also young workers rather than prime age group employees), then constraints on the future supply of secondary workers may be less of a concern.

2 *Qualitative aspects.* Given that most secondary jobs must require little training before recruits become productive, then quality considerations in terms of skill/experience are of relatively little concern to employers – but considerations of reliability, time-keeping etc. remain important. Again, they seem to be secured most readily through changing recruitment sources.

NEW STYLES OF MANAGEMENT?

To put it simply, two sorts of change in work organisation seem to be under way. First, the gap between the conditions of employment of these different groups of worker is widening. At the core, job security, single status conditions and performance-related pay systems contrast with the relatively poor conditions, insecurity and pay levels driven down by competition in the labour market, which are likely to be found among peripheral and external groups. Second, the numerical balance between these groups appears to be changing, with some managers anxious to push as many jobs as possible into peripheral or external categories.

The obvious implication is that a single approach to

manpower management is unlikely to be appropriate to both groups. Nor can it be assumed that conventional forms of management can simply be grafted into any of the emerging groups. Very few of the firms occupied with this work had introduced new management structures, but there was a widespread recognition that changes in emphasis were needed.

Table 2.1 shows how those changes might be structured. For simplicity it concentrates on the opposing ends of the organised spectrum – the core group and the externals. The approach to the two peripheral groups is likely to include elements of both. It can be seen that the focus of the managerial system is quite different for each group: for the core group, the focus is the employee, for the externals the focus is the job. Similarly, the principal form of management control is facilitating the effective deployment of core group workers, an opposed to monitoring delivery of the job against specification for the externals. This might well indicate a participative approach to core group management, compared with a more directive approach to externals.

Table 2.1
Managing the flexible firm

	Core group	Externals
Focus for management	Employee	Job
Instrument of control	Effecting deployment	Delivery against specification
Management style	Participative	Directive
Remuneration system	Wage for time worked	Fee for work done
Motivation/incentive system	Performance appraisal	Delivery on schedule
Supply	Training/recruitment	Competitive tender/severance

Table 2.1 also shows that these divergent approaches to management need to be supported by different rationales for personnel policy. The basis of employment shifts from a salary based on time worked to a fee for work done (among external groups). Incentive payments vary from performance-related at the core to time-related among externals (e.g. bonus for early delivery, penalty payment for late delivery). Labour supply at the core is assured through the recruitment of potential and the provision of extensive training and retraining facilities; among externals it may be assured through competitive tender, or through the establishment of ex-employees on a new contractual basis.

FLEXIBILITY AND THE EMPLOYEE

It is difficult to avoid the conclusion that the fragmentation of the internal labour market in the way described is likely to have a divisive impact on the labour force. The clear implication for employees is that one man's pay, security and career opportunities will increasingly be secured at the expense of the employment conditions of others, often women, more of whom will find themselves permanently relegated in dead end, insecure and low paid jobs. To the extent that these changes are not simply created by recession, they are likely to persist; and if employers find that substantial benefits can be won in this way, they are likely to spread. The implications for workers are therefore serious and likely to have a lasting impact on the experience of work.

Job and employment security. Within the core group, employees will increasingly enjoy security of employment provided they are both capable of retraining and willing to retrain. Outside it, employment security is reduced, and retraining costs are unlikely to be borne by employers – hence secondary workers are likely to become more job-specific at a time when technology is changing the content of many such jobs. In the external group some workers, notably the self-employed subcontractors, will find themselves without job or employment security, and with the entire responsibility of providing business support and training for themselves.

Promotion and careers. In the core group promotion prospects are favourable. Career development will increasingly depend on mastering and deploying new skills, however. Career movement for secondary workers is likely to depend on movement between employers and will therefore be more restricted. Movement between secondary and primary groups is likely to be restricted, except for cases of delayed recruitment (probation) and public subsidy trainees.

Training. Within firms, new training structures for sustaining a supply of key employees in the core group may need to be developed, as internal career paths which existed in a unitary internal labour market will no longer be available. As already suggested, the training needs of secondary workers, although modest, are not likely to be met from current training structures.

Conditions of employment. For secondary employees (particularly in the second peripheral group), conditions of employment seem likely to deteriorate substantially – payments for non-worked time (holidays, sickness and pension) are likely to be most badly affected. Among primary workers conditions are likely to improve, with the twin aim of creating a homogeneous group of employees and encouraging retention.

Pay. The relation between pay and time worked is likely to change for all groups. For core workers pay will be determined increasingly by individual performance rather than through collective agreement. For the peripheral groups pay is likely to vary more explicitly with hours worked, as employers try to match their labour inputs more precisely to their needs over time. For the externals pay is likely to be influenced by performance, but, in this case, more akin to a 'fee-for-work-done' rather than hours attended. An across-the-board approach to rates for any job is therefore likely to become more difficult to sustain.

Unionisation. Union strength in the workplace is likely to be undermined by the fragmentation of the workforce and by the conditions of employment associated with secondary employment. This implies that unions will need to develop new approaches to collective bargaining and to collective representation. Our discussions suggest that as yet the unions are far from formulating such a response, but that, as it is developed, it is likely to cohere around four main themes, as follows:

1 The establishment of union membership agreements to cover all core group employees.
2 The establishment of significantly improved pay and conditions agreements for core workers in exchange for functional flexibility.
3 The extension of those agreed rates and conditions to peripheral and external groups where common or comparable jobs can be defined.
4 The extension of membership agreements to all peripheral and external groups.

FROM DRIFT TO DRIVE: THE WAY AHEAD

It has already been suggested that UK managers, seeking ways of achieving greater flexibility in their deployment of labour, have been hampered by lack of experience, by a readiness to drift rather than consciously hammer out new strategies, and by a preference for gradualism. In conclusion, we consider some guidelines for managers in approaching the question of flexibility.

A RATIONALE FOR FLEXIBILITY

In our experience many UK managers were unclear precisely why they sought greater flexibility. We found at least three rationales, two of which might be regarded with some suspicion, and which appear unlikely to provide a long-term basis for a manpower strategy.

The 'let's put it all out to contract' school of management, which holds that there is necessarily some intrinsic advantage in externalising business activities, was frequently encountered on this research. What such managers were attempting to achieve through outsourcing was not numerical flexibility but functional flexibility – the classic example here would be privatisation among local authority direct works or refuse collection departments, where the aim of externalisation is not to allow for unpredictable fluctuations in workload, but to achieve new working practices and higher productivity. This succeeds in 'making it somebody else's problem' but begs the question of why contractors should be any better at deploying labour than the organisation itself. Exporting an industrial relations problem may be attractive in the short term, but it is unlikely to represent a long-term solution to low productivity. The externalisation of activities should be determined according to the necessary attributes of the job in question rather than contingent attributes.

A second rationale, favoured by some of our respondents, was that reorganisation into peripheral and external groups permitted the reduction of labour costs – particularly through the use of labour with lower on-costs (pension contributions, sick pay, etc.) such as part-time women workers or casual staff. Once again, while this may be an apparently attractive proposition to employers, we found some doubts on this score. The use of cheap labour was widely interpreted by our union respondents as a possible threat to core group workers through undercutting and displacing them. There was some danger here that the use of cheap labour in the periphery might, therefore, undermine the co-operation of core group workers in change rather than help to provide it. As a result, we would have some doubts on the utility of cheap labour strategies, particularly while labour costs can nevertheless be cut through numerical flexibility. If there is a rationale to be found here, then it is in the cheap use of labour (i.e. using only as much labour as required) rather than the use of cheap labour.

Of course, the most important rationale is that reorganisation for flexibility permits and promotes the development of a high productivity, high co-operation and highly flexible core group, which is both capable of and willing to respond positively to change. There may be other rationales for peripheral and external groups, but their main role lies in creating the conditions (of employment security and mutual commitment) required for effective core operations. Therefore the main orientation of any manpower strategy aimed at achieving greater flexibility should begin from defining, developing and facilitating the effective deployment of the core group.

COMBINATION OF THE GROUPS

The diversity of practices between different sectors in their deployment of the different groups has already been referred to. Further, our research suggests that manpower strategies may well differ between otherwise apparently similar firms. The key to inter-firm variation appears to be the different business strategies of the firms in question. For example, one insurance firm interviewed was rapidly expanding its employment of external commission-only salesmen as a means of achieving wide market coverage for its off-the-peg life assurance policies; a second similar firm, concentrating on long term relations with its clients through custom-built policies, was concentrating on a salaried core group salesforce to achieve its business plans. Environmental differences can also be important considerations: for example, a national transport organisation which contributed to this work was faced with quite different manning strategies for its repair and maintenance activities in urban conurbations and commuter suburbs than those which it favoured for geographically remote and disparate areas. Their decisions must be based solely on what is appropriate for their current and anticipated activities. In short, what is required is the creative integration of manpower and business strategies.

MANNING UP

Allocation of activities to particular groups is likely to be on the basis of the characteristics of the posts rather than of the postholders. Yet for the core group worker it is the individual employee's characteristics (versatility, adaption, commitment to the aims of the firm, etc.) which are of greater importance than those of the job (indeed, the very idea of functional flexibility precludes any fixed notion of job definition). The problem faced by firms is, therefore, how to ensure that jobs (particularly in the core) are filled by the right sort of worker.

Some of them already will be, of course; but for those which are not there is an evident need for a new approach to recruitment, selection and training (to get the right ones in) and a more selective approach to severance (to get the wrong ones out). Our research has not been sufficient to do more than identify these needs. We are not therefore in a position to indicate what such new approaches might comprise. It is possible to make some statements – such as, 'recruitment to the core via peripheral jobs is likely to be a better method of selection than direct recruitment', and 'training policies will need to centre less on how to do it than on how to find out how to do it', and 'selective severance policies will need to concentrate more on non-financial assistance and compensation than they have in the past if they are to be successful', and so on. But essentially such new policies need to be developed by employers before they can be adequately researched. It must be sufficient at this stage to identify the need for them.

3 Flexible manning*

Michael Cross

New flexible manning arrangements, particularly the use of contractors, may now help companies cope more efficiently with fluctuating markets.

During the past 5 years or so it has become increasingly apparent that the internal employment systems of many companies are not capable of adapting to rapid economic and technical change. The need to change the span and quantity of competencies of a company's human resources to match the requirements of the market and new technologies has resulted in a need to rethink how people are employed, organised and developed. In some companies the realisation of the need to change organisational structure, managerial style, company culture and conditions of employment is total. These companies are embarking upon long-term programmes of restructuring with the broad objective of increasing the cost-effective use of human resources, strengthening site and business identity, developing team-based commitment to the objectives of the business, eliminating all artificial divisions between employee groups, and generally improving the quality of working life and employee relations. It is with these developments that this chapter is concerned.

Our examination of some of the developments of new job boundaries and organisational structures is divided into five

*This chapter is based on material collected over the period 1981 to 1984 and is summarised in *Towards the Flexible Craftsman*, Technical Change Centre, London.

sections. The first covers the economic and technical factors which are creating pressures and influencing the direction in which jobs and organisations might change. In the second a number of general implications for organisations are outlined, and the elements of old and new organisations are compared. In the third section the broad organisational changes described above are broken down into objectives and principles, which can then be made operational. The fourth section describes the steps taken towards developing flexible manning arrangements, with specific reference to contract staff. In the final section a few thoughts are offered on where the current trends might lead and their implications.

ECONOMIC AND TECHNICAL PRESSURE FOR CHANGE

A few key factors are together creating the need to rethink job boundaries, organisational structures and employment practices. On the economic side the following factors are significant in most industries for causing a change in the approach to employment practices:

1 Increased competition from both UK and non-UK producers in a static or declining market with gross production overcapacity.
2 Stable or near stable prices commanded by finished products has increased pressure to reduce input costs.
3 High and increasing energy costs have required investment to use energy more efficiently and increased the pressure to reduce other input costs.
4 Introduction of cheaper and more versatile substitute products, e.g. PET used instead of glass for soft-drink containers.
5 Changing structure of market for a product, e.g. the growth of contract packaging companies and of multiple retailers has had a significant impact upon the sales of mature packaging materials.
6 Fight for independence to avoid survival mergers/take-overs.

7 Rise in earnings in excess of productivity in UK, which is the reverse of developments in the US and Europe.

Meanwhile on the technical side there are a range of factors forcing companies to rethink the way they manage production and ancillary services. The introduction of the newest equipment has tended to become more frequent in order that firms may compete. This in turn has created a need to develop means of successfully introducing new plant and equipment, often into old environments. In all, there are six particularly significant technical developments which can be identified as affecting the production technologies of most manufacturing companies.

1 The processes have steadily become more complex and expensive.
2 The hardware operated to carry out the processes has become increasingly multi-disciplinary, creating a need for a systems approach to its maintenance and operation. It is thus becoming less obvious and understandable how anything works and interacts, let alone how first to visualise and confirm why it does or does not, or how to improve or alter it. These problems will be offset only partly by modularisation and more sophisticated monitoring, and self-diagnostic systems, themselves add complexity.
3 The manufacturing systems have become increasingly complex and integrated.
4 Control and process engineering requirements have increased in importance.
5 Technological developments in customers' processes are leading to the requirements for tighter specification of product quality control by the producer.
6 Integrated circuits are becoming more complex, sophisticated, and, once programmed, 'intelligent'; and the equipment into which they are built also acquires these characteristics.

Together these developments in technology are directly creating a need to change some of the current ways of working, and in a less direct fashion also offering the opportunity to rethink the allocation of responsibility in organisations. There are three particularly significant developments here:

1 The multi-disciplinary understanding of mixed technology machines and their place within manufacturing systems. This calls into question the craft–craft interface.
2 The multi-role way of working, covering a wide range of tasks which would be traditionally termed skilled and unskilled, or perhaps maintenance and production tasks. This calls into question the craft–process interface.
3 The combining of decision-making (technical) knowledge and the ability to act either within single jobs or in small groups and teams. This calls into question the works–staff interface.

As a result of both economic and technical changes, many existing job and organisational boundaries are called into question, and, if left unchanged, would result in organisational inefficiency and wasted human talent. It is therefore imperative that organisational changes are introduced to allow new competencies to be introduced and developed.

ORGANISATIONS FOR TOMORROW*

Table 3.1 sets out the key features of both traditional and new organisational structures. The traditional organisation follows the technological imperative which regards employees simply as an extension of the machine and therefore as an expendable spare part. By contrast, the new organisation is founded on the principle of joint-optimisation, which regards employees as complementary to the machine and values their unique capabilities for appreciative and evaluative judgement. Employees are therefore a resource to be developed for their own sake rather than to be degraded and cast aside.

It is of specific importance that traditional organisations

---

*This section is based on 'Adapting to a Changing World'; paper presented by Eric Trist at the Sixth International Personnel Conference, Montreal, Canada, November 1977.

are characterised by maximum task-breakdown, which leads to circumscribed job descriptions and single skills – the narrower the better. Employees in such roles are often unable (and unwilling) to manage the uncertainty or the variance that characterises most internal and external company environments. In the traditional organisation layer upon layer of supervision has developed, supported by a wide variety of specialist staffs and formal procedures. The result is a pyramidal structure which tends towards an autocratic management style, even where the paternalism is benign. By contrast, the new organisation is based on an optimum task grouping, which encourages multiple broad-ranging skills. Employees in such a system become capable of a much greater degree of internal control, having flexible group resources to meet a greater degree of change in local circumstances. This leads to a flatter organisational structure characterised by as much lateral as vertical communication. Moreover, it requires a participative management style, with

Table 3.1
Features of traditional and new organisations

Traditional	New
The technological imperative	Joint optimisation
Man as an extension of the machine	Man as complementary to the machine
An expendable spare part	A resource to be developed
Maximum task-breakdown, single narrow skills	Optimum task grouping, multiple broad skills
External controls (supervisors, specialist staffs, procedures)	Internal controls (self-regulating sub-systems)
Tall organisation chart, autocratic style	Flat organisational chart, participative style
Competition, gamesmanship	Collaboration, collegiality
Organisation's purposes only	Members' and society's purposes also
Alienation	Commitment
Low risk-taking	Innovation

the various levels mutually articulated rather than arranged in a simple hierarchy.

SETTING OBJECTIVES AND PRINCIPLES

It is relatively easy to identify with aspects of the move from the old to the new organisation. What is difficult is to appreciate the shift in organisational philosophy, and, furthermore, translate it into objectives and principles with the central aim of developing adaptive and flexible manning arrangements.

As regards the objectives of a programme of organisational change, the following might emerge as being realistic ones:

1 Employment structures, systems and working practices aimed at increased cost-effectiveness in the use and development of human resources.
2 Stronger site and business identity.
3 Team-based commitment to the objectives of the business.
4 Elimination of artificial divisions between employee groups.
5 Improvement in the quality of industrial relations.

The next step is to refine these broad objectives into a number of main principles which identify more specific areas for action. Such a list of main principles for many companies might include the following:

1 Single integrated pay structure based on common job evaluation arrangements, jointly operated; and multi-union negotiations on pay and conditions.
2 Job structures and design enabling optimum flexibility and mobility.
3 Proper relativities.
4 Common philosophy of employment contract, i.e. commitment to a broad range of tasks in return for an annual salary without per occasion payments.
5 The best organisation of working time, and elimination of payment for overtime working.

6 Harmonisation of terms and conditions.
7 A pay structure which is simple to understand, common to all groups, low on administration costs, to provide progression for individuals and accommodate change.
8 Development of full consultative arrangements.

Of the eight main principles listed above, the second one is of particular relevance. It can be developed with specific reference to the changing relation between engineering/maintenance and production departments and their associated job boundaries. In most companies these departments have five potential areas for change. These are the following:

1 Craft/craft interfaces, e.g. fitter/plumber/rigger interfaces and fitter/instrument interfaces.
2 Craft/non-craft interfaces, e.g. fitter/production and instrument/production interfaces.
3 Craft/planner/supervisor interfaces.
4 Craft/craft assistant interfaces.
5 Craft/other activities, e.g. cleaners and civil trades.

It is these boundaries and interfaces which are currently being modified through increased flexibility, the integration of existing jobs, and changes in organisational structure. In all these changes are giving rise to:

1 The development of core mechanical and instrument/electrical jobs through the grouping and combination of existing trades. In time, this leads to a composite, non-trade designed craft job.
2 A rethinking of the engineering specialisms and support services needed full-time on site, and an examination of the best way of providing them, either by contractors or by a company's own personnel (see Figure 3.1).

The division of work into core (fixed labour costs) and non-core (variable labour costs) activities highlights the possible role of contractors for undertaking many specialist and non-essential jobs. A number of these developments are illustrated in the next section.

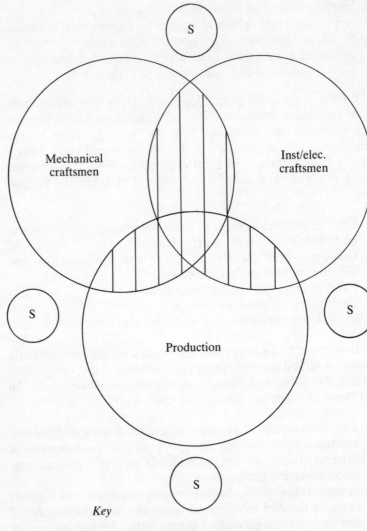

Key

S = support activities
Large circles = core activities
Small circles = non-core activities
Shaded areas = scope for further changes

Figure 3.1   Core and non-core engineering and production activities

EXAMPLES OF FLEXIBLE MANNING

While there is general agreement about the direction the management of companies should take in seeking to develop new working practices, progress is usually relatively slow. The typical steps taken (both with, and without agreement of the local unions) towards developing more flexible manning arrangements are fourfold:

1 General reduction in the numbers employed in all trades, especially among the fabricating, civil and other ancillary trades, and craft (unskilled and semi-skilled) assistants.
2 A move to promote core trades to form mechanical and electrical/instrument craft jobs through a series of productivity/flexibility agreements. In addition, the introduction of a division between frontline maintenance and central engineering services.
3 A move to combine production and frontline maintenance engineering and technical resources under a common management/supervisory structure. This may be done possibly through the forming of multi-skilled teams, made-up of still predominantly single-disciplined craftsmen and production workers.
4 Still further integration of production and frontline maintenance resources through the development of multi-disciplinary multi-role craftsmen (in part through direct entry from apprenticeships/traineeships), and also through the emergence of user–maintainer jobs in some instances. This latter development is in part being encouraged by the current high levels of unemployment among craftsmen who are applying for production jobs, and so seeds are being sown for future moves to integrate production and frontline maintenance. Other engineering and technical resources devoted to planned and scheduled maintenance (the management of which might be transferred to production), such as plant overhauls and installation, and specialist technical support, can be supplemented and even replaced by contract staff.

These four steps should be regarded as a very general

description of the moves made towards introducing flexible and integrated manning practices and an appropriate organisation structure across a whole series of industries.

Most of the attention and effort at the present time is focused upon the development of flexible manning arrangements which encourage skill and knowledge interchange across the interfaces noted earlier. As a result of these efforts, the possibility of using contract staff is becoming an increasingly important consideration for several main types of work. These are the following:

1 *Civil trades work*, e.g. painting, plumbing, bricklaying, joinery, etc. Many of these jobs will be undertaken by existing craftsmen or any remaining handymen, unless the workload is sufficient to justify the use of contract staff.
2 *Plant shutdowns and overhauls*. These are events which are planned and usually require large numbers of craftsmen to work on a specific plant (or plants') turnarounds for several weeks or more. Even on the largest sites in the UK there is rarely sufficient work to justify the employment of a full complement of craftsmen on a continuous basis. For this type of work there is potential for the greater use of contract staff, notwithstanding the local barriers to pursuing this strategy. The more routine pump and value overhauls, for example, are becoming less frequent and skill-intensive as a result of changes in design and materials used in their construction, and this also encourages the use of outside contract staff.
3 *Capital projects*, e.g. plant installation and engineering commissioning. These projects are already frequently carried out by the suppliers and engineering construction and fabricating companies. It is possible that, given the downturn in the number of large capital projects in the UK, they might take on in the overhaul of petrochemical, chemical and oil refining plants (see 2 above).
4 *Specialist technical support*, e.g. computer and process control maintenance support and highly specialised welding work. In the UK food-processing industry, for example, approximately 40 per cent of establishments are using some form of microelectronics-based process

control equipment. Of this 40 per cent, nearly half (47 per cent) are making use of a maintenance and repair service provided by the equipment manufacturer or supplier. How long term this development will be is difficult to assess, but, given the present level of retraining and recruitment to meet the skill and knowledge requirements of process control systems, the use of outside (contract) assistance will decline.

Of these four categories of contract work, the two which are of particular significance are contract labour for plant shutdowns and overhauls, and for the maintenance and service of equipment and work requiring specialist skills and knowledge.

However, there are a number of potential barriers to the possible benefits of making increased use of contract staff. These are:

1 *Cost.* While there are many short-term cost savings to be made by using contract staff, in the long term the costs might exceed those of employing the equivalent number of people on a permanent basis. The general view is that, while there may be a disparity between the short- and long-term costs of using contract staff, it makes sound commercial sense to keep the permanent employment base at a minimum because of the costs and difficulties of adjusting to future changes in the market. Leaving aside this view, there is also the absolute cost of using contract staff, which can be reduced as the necessary skills and knowledge are acquired in-house.

2 *Quality.* There is always a question mark hanging over contract staff's competency and safety standards, which are often difficult to monitor. While inferior workmanship can be corrected under the terms and conditions of any service contract or similar, it can prove very costly to do so. It would appear this view has developed at least in part because of the lack of a well developed contracting industry in the UK. Consequently, when contract staff are used, it is likely that they have not been able to develop the necessary in-depth competencies to handle specific

overhaul contracts. This situation reflects the lack of a developed market for their services, and also the relatively small scale of the UK industrial market for such services, even if fully developed.

3 *Vulnerability*. There is the feeling, despite the commercial arguments in favour of using contract staff, which favours the manning-up of a plant to meet almost any and every eventuality. But how many 'risks' are companies willing to take? How reliable is the contract service on offer? How much contract cover is required?

4 *Employee relations*. Here there are a series of potential fears and barriers. What work will the contractors be used for? What will be the effect upon the development of the skills and knowledge of existing craftsmen on site? How will union membership and representation be affected? How will overtime work be organised and affected in the future? What will be the effect on the security of employment of the permanent employees in the short and long terms?

At the moment the process of developing the use of contractors is a relatively slow one, except for 'high/new technology', but the direction adopted by companies to date makes the increased use of contract staff almost inevitable.

CONCLUSIONS AND IMPLICATIONS

The trends which are shaping the labour forces of many large manufacturing and processing companies are occurring as a result of commercial, technical and institutional factors, and would appear to be the beginnings of a longer term trend. Many of the current attractions of using contractors will probably decline as some of the complications of relying upon external support are realised. However, despite any complications, it would appear that the use of contractors will increase, though perhaps not to the levels suggested by some observers. Apart from this general comment, there are four specific implications which need to be considered further.

1 *Education and training.* Because of the emerging separation of permanent and contract staffs, it will become increasingly necessary to reconsider both the access to, and content of, existing education and training courses. It is important to note that the key issues here are those of delivery methods and access to relevant training courses. These will require the packaging and combining of much existing material rather than completely starting from scratch, and giving undue emphasis to 'new' technology subjects.

2 *Unions.* There is a major social dilemma facing the main unions representing general and skilled workers. Depending upon the approach adopted for matching job requirements to potential job-holders (i.e. top-down versus bottom-up), there are two distinct messages emerging. The first favours 'giving' maintenance-cum-engineering tasks to production workers, and the second 'giving' production work to engineering craftsmen. It is therefore necessary for the unions concerned, i.e. TGWU, GMBATU, AUEW and EETPU, to resolve this issue among themselves at all levels of their organisations.

3 *Employers.* One of the main requirements in most companies is to develop an equitable method of rewarding all employees, and in particular developing a joint production and engineering pay and grading structure. Another ingredient in the move towards an integrated pay structure is the need to recognise a wider range of skills and attributes than are normally considered relevant to craft and production jobs. A related development will be the move from individual training reviews and counselling to full performance appraisal for production and engineering employees. Each of these developments is seeking to maximise the flexibility and contribution of all employees to performance of a company.

4 *Contractors.* The market for their services in most manufacturing and processing companies will increase over the next few years for non-routine and non-core activities associated with operating and maintaining production units. However, many of the existing 'jobs' which would appear prime candidates for contracting out will

probably cease to exist altogether, being shared out among the core group of workers. Such 'jobs' include painting, bricklaying, rigging etc. Where contractors will continue to make major inroads will be in transportation, catering, security, etc., and to a lesser extent in engineering services.

From these comments and observations it is evident that the use of contractors is a significant development, but that their increased use is only one aspect of the much more significant change in organisational structure and management style which is aimed at achieving greater flexibility and integration at the workplace.

4 Linked subcontracting

David Clutterbuck

In Europe and the USA companies are beginning to shed employees, then rehire them as independent contractors.

Juan Carlos Grijelbo, chairman of Spanish printers Artes Graficas S.A., cured his biggest headache when he sold the company's trouble-laden photocomposition department to the employees. Then he took its services back again – as an independent subcontractor.

'Now, only 18 people produce double the amount of work that 53 employees did before, when they were on the staff,' Grijelbo says.

The Spanish printing firm is just one of a growing number of companies questioning the traditional concept of permanent employment, and discovering the benefits of turning employees into suppliers. In industries ranging from chemicals and computing to forestry and electronic assembly, European and US companies are finding that paying by commercial contract instead of by salary can reduce overheads while increasing productivity. They are also finding that many employees, far from resisting being cast out from the corporate womb, welcome the independence they are offered.

'Contracting-out', as the practice is called, allows the employer to trim his headcount without sacrificing the valuable and sometimes irreplaceable talents and background knowledge of skilled employees.

This was a strong element in the reasoning behind the deal Britain's Imperial Chemical Industries (ICI) recently made

with two computer experts in its plastics research labora-
tories. ICI is in the midst of a major rationalisation that
involves consolidating its plastics activities in the north-east
of England, and closing down much of its research at
Welwyn Garden City, near London. Neither John Simons
nor his colleague Paul Davis liked the idea of going north.
Instead they proposed setting up their own company,
Parkway Computer Consultants.

ICI's local resettlement manager, Gordon Libretto,
responded enthusiastically. However, it quickly became
clear that Davis would be needed for some time to complete
a major project he had started, to automate laboratory
testing procedures. In late 1982, the two computer specialists were 'seconded' to their own firm, for a year, and given a
$30,000 contract to complete the project Davis had been
working on. 'He charges us commercial rates and we claw
back his salary,' explains Libretto. At the end of 1984 both
men formally ceased to be employees, received their
severance pay-off, and became just another supplier to ICI –
albeit with the promise of preferential treatment.

Knowledge of the people and the inside workings of the
group has helped the two entrepreneurs pick up business
from other divisions of ICI and they have also begun to
attract major outside orders, to the extent that they have
taken on part-time staff to help them.

One of the first ICI employees to forge a contracting-out
deal was Ronald Foord, formerly a buyer at the company's
paints division. When the division decided to close down a
satellite office in Slough, some 45 km west of London, it was
left with the dilemma of what to do with the print-shop that
had been housed there. Foord, who had responsibility for
the print-shop and its thirteen employees, put his redundancy money into renting new premises and taking over the
unit as his own company, Kent Chase Ltd, in the autumn of
1976.

'ICI wanted to cut peripheral activities, but it didn't want
to lose access to printing,' he says. 'It gave me a short-term
loan, a three-year contract and advantageous payment terms
on the equipment I took with me. I give them what another
printer can't – background knowledge of the company.'

The amount of work for ICI has stayed steady at about $185,000 annually, while Foord has built up other sources to provide work of about the same value. 'I now have 10 employees,' says Foord, 'doing twice the volume of work.'

Finnish paper manufacturer Enso-Gutzeit Oy has had similar increases in productivity in its forestry operations where in 1980 it sold the log-hauling tractors to its drivers, on preferential loan terms. All the drivers paid back their loans within three years, so Enso was encouraged to sell 18 of its giant tree harvesters (mobile machines which pluck, strip and chop up a tree within 40 seconds) to its operators on the same conditions.

FEWER MANAGERS NEEDED

Enso's motivation came from the skyrocketing costs of labour and frequent equipment breakdowns in the forestry operation, which made the return on capital from the machines very poor. Since the drivers became their own masters, however, the annual working loads have increased by about 30 per cent. Part of the explanation is that the drivers now take much better care of the machines.

Enso has also found that it requires fewer supervisors to direct the activities of the subcontractors than it did when they were employees, because they are more prepared to take on responsibility for what they do.

Still in Finland, neon light manufacturer Tammerneon was concerned at the low employee morale, work stoppages and production bottlenecks in the small unit that blew the neon tubes – the heart of the manufacturing process. Managing director Markku Koskenniemi looked for a solution that would provide a financial incentive for the employees concerned, who resisted overtime on the grounds that it was not worthwhile when they had to pay high rates of tax. Koskenniemi also wanted a solution that would reduce bureaucracy and increase productivity.

After discussions with the unions and the three employees in the unit, one glass blower was transferred elsewhere in the company and the other two were invited to form their own production company. They now rent space and equipment and purchase raw materials from Tammerneon.

Koskenniemi is pleased because the industrial relations climate has improved dramatically and productivity in the unit has risen 250 per cent. The employees are happy because they arrange their own hours, supervise their own work and reap the rewards of their own productivity. Being self-employed gives them tax advantages, too. The only disagreeable note comes from the tax authority, which regards the scheme as merely another method of tax avoidance.

Artes Graficas' Grijelbo faced comparable production problems in his phototypesetting operation. The heavy investment in equipment was under-used, and productivity was low. In February 1982 the department was spun off as a co-operative, Fotocomposicion Didot, in which Artes Graficas retained only 20 per cent of the shares. The employees who went to the new company took a further 20 per cent, and the rest were bought by managers and some workers in the parent company.

'We never could have dreamed it would turn out so well for both sides,' says Grijelbo. 'Already profits are 60 per cent of the total capital invested in the company, and it has an order book 100 per cent full. They can hardly keep up with the demand.' In fact, Fotocomposicion Didot now has fourteen additional individual subcontractors itself. Instead of being totally reliant on Artes Graficas for its business, it now takes 75 per cent of its order value from outside.

All the employees who joined the new company had the option to return to Artes Graficas if they did not like the change of working environment. None has done so.

Now other Artes Graficas employees have asked if they, too, can form subcontracting companies. 'We are studying plans to segregate the binding operation later this year,' says Grijelbo. 'We expect it to reduce our indirect costs and increase efficiency and productivity dramatically.'

The company that has achieved most international exposure for its enterprising experiments in contracting-out to former employees is Britain's Rank Xerox. It took the unusual step of analysing the real costs of employing people at its London headquarters. It was horrified to discover that, on average, an employee on £10,000 a year salary in 1984 cost an extra £17,000 in support facilities, such as rent, rates, heating, canteen, employment benefits and taxes, travel and data processing. 'We decided', says Philip Judkins, manager of headquarters personnel, 'to cut our costs by keeping the people and getting rid of the facilities.'

Rank Xerox's solution, which it calls networking, calls for employees to leave the company and establish their own limited company. This in turn contracts with Rank Xerox to provide specified services in exchange for a set fee. These services do not comprise more than half the output of the networking company. 'We insist on that maximum,' explains Judkins, 'to maintain the networker's independence. If he does not become an entrepreneur, then we are just featherbedding him, and we see no reason for doing that.'

The office equipment company eases the transition into independence for its employees by career counselling, then training in any specific skills they need to work at home from a microcomputer terminal, connected to company head-quarters by telephone. Since the scheme started in 1981, forty-eight Rank Xerox employees, drawn from all levels from executives to directors, have applied to become networkers. Rank Xerox currently turns down one in two applicants, either because the available job is not suitable, or because, in the opinion of the company, the individual would be better advised to remain as a permanent employee.

'The people who network have a strong need for personal achievement that enhances their productivity,' says Judkins. 'In some cases, if they didn't go with our help, they'd leave and join another company, so we'd lose their skill and expertise anyway.'

At Clydebank in Scotland J. W. Naisby, former security manager at UIE Ltd's shipyard, can also point to remark-able productivity increases since he persuaded the com-pany's board to subcontract security and firefighting to him in 1980. He took with him most of his subordinates and paid them a higher wage in return for giving up sick pay benefits.

'We used to lose 700 days a year through sick leave when

we were all employed directly by the yard,' he says. 'Since I became an independent subcontractor we have lost only 15½ days in total.' At the same time, his workforce has built up from fourteen to nineteen men.

In all these cases the former employees have ended up with more money in their pockets. But in one example from the United States, they willingly accepted *less* pay. Hyatt-Clark Industries, of Clark, New Jersey, was a subsidiary of General Motors (GM) and in deep trouble. GM sold the plant, which makes tapered roller bearings, to the managers and employees, and awarded it a three-year contract to take much of its produce. The workers went along with the plan, which included redundancy for a third of their number, and voted themselves a 30 per cent cut in wages.

Why are people so willing to give up the apparent security of salaried employment with a large company for the perils of small business? One reason may be that the large company is no longer the safe haven it used to be. Many employees decide it is better to provide their own security, through a venture over which they have some personal control. Another reason is that people who feel boxed in by their current jobs can expand into other areas gradually, without having to make a sudden clean break.

In Brussels, management consultant Gunnar Beeth opted out of his job as vice president of the subsidiary of US fishing tackle manufacturers Berkley & Co. because he needed more challenge. He contracted to continue working for the company half time, on half salary, as a consultant. At the same time, he set up his own consultancy, Imaconsult S.A., and began looking for other clients. 'We had losses for the first 18 months but we've been profitable ever since,' he says. Gradually the volume of work he does for Berkley has declined while the work for other clients has grown.

Most of the companies that have made use of this willingness on the part of employees to contract out have been delighted by the peripheral benefits of the arrangement. Although the main intention has usually been to cut overheads or reduce staff levels, the improvement in productivity has frequently become more important.

Another benefit to the large firm is the broader experience

of the contract worker. Says Beeth: 'Working for more than one company, you have access to a wide range of information. An internal person may have the same depth of knowledge, but not the same breadth. You can also be more objective.'

In Belgium the growing popularity of contracting out has much to do with the high indemnities companies have to pay to make employees redundant. Contracting out can be a cheaper option. In addition, points out Bob Gattie, of executive search consultants Tasa Inc.: 'The company's conscience is easier, because the employee avoids the stigma of being unemployed.'

In West Germany, Harry Bolz, of computer services bureau GFU Boeser & Bolz GmbH, was reluctant to discourage employees from setting up in competition. So he offers all employees the choice of working as staffers or as independent consultants. The consultants receive up to 80 per cent of the contract fee and are free to take any other work they can find. Staffers, on the other hand, receive all the normal employee benefits such as holiday pay, annual bonus and social security contributions. According to Bolz, staffers and contract workers cost about the same.

The picture isn't entirely rosy, however. There are snags to the contracting-out movement. Once it has divested key skills, the company that takes the contracting-out route has to accept that the former employees may find more profitable work elsewhere. Rebuilding a skill base may be a costly and time-consuming business. There is also a danger that managers who are used to having direct authority over people may be out of their depth motivating independent contractors. Many will have to improve the clarity of the instructions they give, because the work will not be done on company premises.

For the employees, the risks are much greater. For a start, says Gattie, the employee who contracts out loses all involvement in the power structure of the company. He is also vulnerable to changes of policy or senior personnel. A new chief executive may not feel beholden to arrangements made in the past – indeed, he may make a virtue of sweeping away the hangers-on of a previous administration.

Siemens AG in West Germany, for example, used to make frequent use of former employees as contract computer analysts and programmers. Sometimes a project team would consist of one staff member in charge and up to 10 independent contractors, says one former Siemens employee. Because the contract employees earned more, other salaried employees would quit, only to return to the same desk at higher pay the next day.

Now Siemens has reversed this policy. According to a company spokesman it now goes to the opposite extreme, pulling in full-time staff from as far away as Vienna or Munich to work on projects in Cologne, rather than take on contract labour.

Another problem for contracted out employees comes when the large company suffers from reduced orders.

BRAVE VENTURE FAILED

Such was the case with a group of employees who contracted out all the servicing of refrigerators for Singer Corp.'s French subsidiary. In 1974 Singer decided to get out of refrigerator manufacturing. To do so, however, would have cost it at least $10 million in severance pay and arrangements to continue after-sales service.

The US company came up with the idea of selling the sales operation to the 900 employees, who put up $700,000 between them to form a company called Servifrance. Singer retained one-third of the shares and the Bank Verne took another 5 per cent.

With promises of a 17 per cent dividend, Singer came out of the deal well, especially once it had disposed of all the spare parts to the new company for another $700,000. But the dream soon turned to a nightmare. As the number of Singer refrigerators in use declined, so did business. Other manufacturers still in the market had their own after-sales service organisations. By 1979, the brave venture was forced to file for bankruptcy, and the employees found themselves out of work.

For most of the entrepreneurs, however, the lure of independence with a safety net of limited but guaranteed work is compelling. Alfredo Ribera, formerly an engineer with Olivetti in Spain, set up his own component manufacturing workshop in 1969. Olivetti still provides most of his business. He claims that Olivetti retains his services because he and his employees are more efficient and dynamic than the large company could be if it manufactured the parts itself.

'I work a lot harder, because it's my own company,' he says. 'But I enjoy my work more. And I'm making a lot of money.'

A CASE STUDY by *Pedro Nueno*

THE ENVIRONMENT

General Franco died in 1975. The Spanish economy was still growing with practically no adjustments for the increase in the price of energy. During the second half of the seventies, priority was given to the political processes of creating a democracy: legalisation of political parties and unions, development of a constitution, democratic elections, and – peculiar to Spain – an important process of decentralisation with the rise of autonomous governments in several regions.

The international recession and the establishment of a democracy proved costly, and the business environment went quickly from high growth to stagnation: from less than 10 per cent inflation to close to 30 per cent; from negative to positive interest rates; from low to high taxation; from a peaceful and productive labour force to labour unrest, millions of working hours lost, and labour costs growing faster than inflation; from a protected economy to a gradually more liberalised one; from a strong peseta to a drastic devaluation. But most managers continued to think in terms of a growth economy, introducing only short-term remedies and waiting for less turbulent times, which they expected would come soon.

INDUSTRIAL RECONVERSION

The 1980s brought clear evidence that many companies in the Spanish economy had to go through a process of adjustment to the new conditions of the domestic environment. The issue of 'Industrial Reconversion' became popular, and government, employers and labour unions implicitly agreed that something would have to be done to help industry to regain competitiveness.

Under certain conditions labour unions would be more willing to accept lay-offs in order to prevent bankruptcies and thus to preserve a portion of the jobs; governments – both at national and regional levels – would be willing to offer special help to companies submitting feasibility studies for reconversion projects; owners of companies were willing to bring more equity in some instances, reduce their ownership in other cases and, very often, strengthen their management teams. Not surprisingly, consultants, auditors and head hunters prospered in Spain in the 1980s.

While such politically influential industries as shipbuilding, steel, and electronics received special attention and pushed their respective reconversion plans through with a great deal of government support, most of Spanish industry, comprising thousands of medium sized and small companies, had to go ahead with its own reconversion plans with little help from the central government. (It must be said that regional autonomous governments paid more attention to this important segment of the economy, and in the regions where these governments had achieved some degree of operating capability – basically Catalonia and the Basque country – many medium and small companies benefited also from some public help for their reconversion projects.)

Suspension of payments (a legal device that allows a company to reach a special agreement with its debtors, delaying its payments) and bankruptcies were frequent, and the number of unemployed grew fast to about 2.5 millions, over 20 per cent of the labour force, in 1984, as companies fought for survival and productivity. What happened inside these companies? We shall look at this in some detail.

NORTHERN PRINTING, A TYPICAL MEDIUM SIZED SPANISH COMPANY

The company that we shall call Northern Printing had been founded early in this century in one of the industrial cities of the Basque country. At the end of the 1970s the company was still owned and managed by the sons of the founder; they were between 50 and 70 years old, though a few members of the third generation had just joined the company and had been assigned staff responsibilities. The company employed 430 people and produced all types of printed materials, from high quality books to posters, and from cheque books to encyclopedias. Northern Printing had achieved a reputation as the industry leader in quality, and its products sold all over the country and abroad. Traditionally, the company had been able to sell at prices higher than the industry averages on the basis of its superior quality. Customers had been willing to accept the not absolutely reliable delivery dates of Northern Printing, but the company, in turn, had always accepted late changes in the specifications of the products to be printed (in some cases even after the printing process had started), and had not pressed its customers for collection of receivables.

One of the brothers, the eldest, acted as president and handled process technology. Another brother was in charge of sales, supervising half a dozen salesmen but making most of the sales himself on the basis of long-standing personal relationships, trust and service orientation. The third brother, the youngest, was in charge of production. Finance and accounting had been for many years second level functions at Northern Printing, left to more or less qualified clerks. The company had always made money and had provided an excellent standard of living to the owner–managers and their large families.

Technical advance had the highest priority at Northern Printing. The company had pioneered computer applications in the several phases of the printing process and had invested in advanced equipment. Most managers and supervisors were highly qualified technicians. The internal environment had a very professional look, with well-educated, well-dressed men often meeting in large groups, plenty of computer screens and keyboards, and high quality products being processed.

The late 1970s, however, brought surprising market changes: it shrank and became more price-conscious; small companies specialising in one product were able to offer better prices and service; lower quality publications were produced, with publishers shifting towards more reprints and less sophisticated productions. Combined with these new market trends, the environmental changes described earlier started to produce unpleasant evidence of trouble: cash pressures increased, backlogs decreased and customers became more demanding.

A young MBA was then hired as financial manager and one of the members of the third generation, Mr Andoni Gorosti, also an MBA graduate, was asked to prepare a report on the company situation and prospects. The combined study of Mr Gorosti and the new financial manager was very alarming: the productivity of Northern Printing was very low, the company was operating below breakeven point, it had been losing money during the past two years, and internal operations were difficult to control (accounting was unreliable and most operations depended upon personal contacts and relations, word of mouth and tradition).

Alternatives considered

After careful evaluation of the report described above and long discussions, the three owner–managers accepted the situation and Mr Gorosti was appointed general manager of Northern Printing, with a free hand to turn the company around. Mr Gorosti hired two additional professional managers, both of them MBA graduates also, who were put in charge of sales and production. He kept on the older generation (his father and two uncles) but gradually transferred operating responsibilities from them to the new management team. One year after he took over as general manager, Mr Gorosti had a reliable picture of the situation both internally and in the market, and had established control mechanisms. Meanwhile he had informed the workers' committee of the difficult situation of the company, and secured their support in the salvage operation. In addition, he had reached an agreement with the employees, and those who wished could take early retirement or leave the company with a reasonable indemnity.

Mr Gorosti and his management team set themselves the following objectives:

1 To implement a strong sales effort in Spain and in the export markets, in order to increase the level of output with the current labour force, thereby improving productivity.

2 To cut the number of employees, transforming Northern Printing into a smaller but more efficient company.
3 To focus on one or a few product lines where high efficiency could be achieved, divesting the company of unnecessary assets and laying off redundant employees.

The chosen path

Careful analysis led them to the decision to cut back. The tough situation in the domestic market, plus the uncertainty of the Latin American market (traditionally a good market for Spanish publishers and printers), meant that a productivity-through-growth alternative was risky. The fact that the product line of the company was wide, with no single product group accounting for more than 25 per cent of sales, made the focus alternative a difficult choice, because the company would have had to undergo too much surgery.

The management team then carried out a detailed study, evaluating the jobs of each manager, supervisory or worker in the company. The result of this study indicated that one-third of the employees would not be necessary if the remainder worked with a reasonable level of productivity. At least one-third of the redundant employees were indirect workers or supervisory personnel.

A tough period of discussion with the workers' committee and with the persons facing redundancy followed this analysis. The process of reducing the company's size was started with determination. But Mr Gorosti was always concerned with the enormous complexity of a vertically integrated printing process, with numerous operations difficult to measure, schedule, and control. Moreover, he was worried about the motivation of employees after the painful trimming exercise. Finally he developed a new concept for his company – not as a vertically integrated unit, but as a group of small units, each one specialising in one of the sub-processes of printing. He decided to test the concept by spinning-off one of the most controversial subprocesses – composition. In this process, manuscripts, photographs and graphics are made up in the form of punched tape, computer tape or film, and one of those will be the basis for the production of the printing plates.

Since some clients supplied their composition already made up, there were some easy jobs. However, there were also some extremely difficult jobs, for example when clients wanted only the composition of a given publication. Consequently, the operation of this department was the most difficult to schedule and control. Mr Gorosti decided to make an investment, buying the best and most automated composition equipment available. He then persuaded his composition department manager to become general manager of a newly formed company which would specialise only in composition. (He thought this man had great managerial potential; he was a leader, and once he accepted the new job, it would be easier to convince other employees to follow.) He created a board of directors for the new company and on it he put his three senior managers, plus the general manager of the new company; each also received a 10 per cent equity stake in the new venture. The newly created company would work for Northern Printing, which would be the parent company, but not exclusively. It could work for other companies too.

The composition company was created and twenty-five people (about half the employees who worked in Northern Printing's composition department) were offered and accepted a transfer to it. The concept proved very successful, and 6 months later the new company was enjoying a strong cash flow that was allowing it to pay for its equipment and to distribute some dividends.

Mr Gorosti decided then to pursue this strategy aggressively and to spin-off department after department, following the same model. Where he could not find anyone inside Northern Printing suitable for the general managership of a spin-off subsidiary, he would hire an outsider. His key executives would take their places on the boards of all the companies created. Northern Printing would centralise sales, finance and control, but the general managers of the subsidiaries would be encouraged to interest themselves in sales, and purchasing, production, and personnel management would be their responsibility.

By 1984, practically all the departments of Northern Printing had been spun off as independent companies (composing, printing, binding, etc.). The sales level had increased, and the number of employees was close to half the original size. Each independent company was run efficiently and flexibly, with selected workers and very limited supervision. Overheads had been reduced sharply.

From the financial standpoint, some of the companies created required little more than a set of book entries, since Northern Printing received shares in the spin-off subsidiaries in exchange for equipment. Other companies required some investment but this was made at the expense of the parent company (for example, all new companies went to rented space, but Northern Printing owned well-located buildings that, as they were emptied by the departing companies, were sold).

By 1984 it had become evident to managers and employees in the group of companies created that Northern Printing was going to survive and succeed.

A final comment

Northern Printing is an example among many small and medium sized Spanish companies that have chosen this approach to reconvert themselves. In certain instances this process has led to an increase in the submerged or underground economy: a company has given birth to a variety of smaller units and then it has liquidated or gone bankrupt. The newly created units may employ some people who at the same time receive unemployment benefits and are willing to work illegally, and part of the exchanges between these small units may take the form of barter or 'cash' transfers, thus escaping fiscal control. The government has turned a blind eye on these irregularities, probably because the new companies provide some social relief in industrialised areas with high unemployment, and because they may be the seed of companies that at some point will organise themselves on a more orthodox basis.

There is no doubt, however, that the concept of spin-offs has the potential to increase efficiency, competitiveness and innovation through focused management, simplification, and increased autonomy at lower levels.

5 Meaning business: values in the workplace

Dennis Bumstead and *John Eckblad*

Companies are moving in a new direction as they reassess their own motives and principles of action. However, they must develop their business cultures responsibly, since many employees are easily manipulated by the authority and values of a company.

During our current post-industrial revolution, as we find our way through the transition from an industrial society to a society based upon information, it is not surprising that there is a resurgence of interest in the importance of values, meaning and purpose in shaping the development of companies. The old order of full employment, moderate growth and relatively stable international economic demarcations is breaking down. Old businesses collapse. New ones spring up, but some of those, like Laker Airways or Osborne Computers, fail to put down roots and flower only briefly. The way forward is far from clear.

In this context, some managers realise that they need to take a fresh look at fundamental questions. What business are we really in? What do we stand for as an organisation? What is the meaning of our activities? To what ends are our managerial and technical competencies directed? We have evidence from *In Search of Excellence* (Peters and Waterman, 1982) that attention to these questions is a central feature of the behaviour of a significant number of successful companies. We have strong evidence that dealing with these questions is at the heart of many of the companies that have created 'the Japanese miracle' (see e.g. Pascale and Athos, 1981). We also have the widely identified motivational problems in organisations and society (see e.g. Handy 1978, Lessem 1982, Robertson 1983), an important aspect of which is the desire of many people for an increased sense of meaning and purpose in their lives. And of course, we have the learned testimony of Cleese *et al.* making a joke out of the subject ('Monty Python's The Meaning of Life'), which must mean that it is important to our time.

To the extent that in addressing these questions companies go beyond dusting off the statement of company philosophy which served its purpose for the last 20 or 30 years, they are dealing with very powerful energies. As we shall see, the 'excellent companies' study and the Japanese experience seem to suggest that not only are the questions worthwhile in their own right but also the powerful energies associated with them can be channelled to good effect in terms of conventional success criteria. We shall explore some of the potential pitfalls, particularly the dangers of fanaticism, of misusing powerful appeals to values and purpose. And we shall look at some evidence that this kind of misuse can occur not only in dramatic political settings but also in deceptively ordinary circumstances.

Elsewhere (Bumstead, 1983) it has been argued that overcoming the current economic crisis will require large organisations to adopt a 'paedomorphic' strategy – 'change through small organisational forms'. The organisations which remain centralised and monolithic will be the dinosaurs of our age. Those which decentralise and encourage semi-autonomous new ventures in parallel with their existing mainstream business will have much better chances of evolving effectively. Of course this does not imply abdication at the centre. Effective leadership of a relatively decentralised organisation is actually more challenging, since it requires a confident and subtle combination of vision, clarity of objectives *and* trust in local management, manifested by not interfering with the specifics of local activities.

The exploration and clarification of meaning and values are integral to this. The most unproductive outcome of the current interest in corporate values – very likely in some companies – would be a top-down attempt to put across particular values. The worst of the worst would be to try to adopt Japanese values or those of some of the excellent American companies and transmit them down the organisation. Such an approach is liable to be either an ineffective waste of energy or, with the 'right' combination of internal selling techniques applied to it, positively dangerous. The danger in such an approach is that it results in people behaving over-zealously in the name of the organisation and its new values.

Rather than this, what is needed is a managed, decentralised exploration of values. This should be firmly grounded in the Western traditions of freedom, self-determination and empiricism. A sufficiently confident senior management should explore its own values and its views of what the company stands for. It should, at the same time, encourage and enable such exploration to take place around the organisation. Enabling such a process to take place is an example of an extremely demanding decentralised management task. The activity must be sufficiently decoupled from normal hierarchical controls that people can genuinely have room to explore the issues. It must avoid becoming a command performance.

In practice the process is most likely to succeed on the basis of local initiatives which emphasise self-development. Quite a number of such initiatives are to be found inside organisations, usually proceeding in a relatively quiet and unheralded fashion. Building gradually on these is the best chance of taking the first steps towards enabling an organisation to clarify its values and accept its diversity. This can provide a basis for the sense of personal and organisational meaning that is so fundamental to high quality business.

MEANING IN 'EXCELLENT' COMPANIES

In their influential study *In Search of Excellence: Lessons from America's Best-Run Companies* (1982), Peters and Waterman state: 'Every excellent company we studied is clear on what it stands for and takes the process of value shaping seriously. In fact, we wonder whether it is possible to be an excellent company without clarity on values and without having the right sort of values' (p.280).

They acknowledge that many people in business have difficulty in talking about this subject – and we may speculate that perhaps this difficulty is greater, even, in Europe than America. There are good reasons for some caution in this area. Nonetheless, Peters and Waterman found that virtually all their better performing companies had well defined sets of shared values or guiding beliefs. The lesser performers either had no set of coherent beliefs or they focused almost exclusively on conventional, quantifiable financial objectives such as earnings per share, return on investment, market share and the like. 'Ironically, the companies . . . with the most precise financial targets – had done *less* well financially than those with broader, less precise, more qualitative statements of corporate purpose' (Peters and Waterman, p.281). There is, of course, no suggestion that the better performers abandoned conventional, quantitative objectives – only that these were *treated as important but secondary*.

Peters and Waterman go on to indicate several features of the value centrality of their excellent companies. Firstly, there is the importance the top leadership of the company attaches to its part in articulating and reinforcing the guiding beliefs. Secondly, they found that these beliefs were disseminated and kept alive by stories, myths, legends and metaphors which circulated informally around these organisations. Thirdly, they point out that the beliefs were not simply 'motherhood' statements about right and wrong. Rather they were linked to the central functions of each organisation. So, for example, in Johnson and Johnson the stories tend to be quality stories, in 3M they are innovation stories, at Delta Airlines they frequently concern customer service. Fourthly, the central values are spelled out at a general, abstract level *and* shown to be directly relevant to grounded, operational decisions. Finally, this values orientation does not constitute a boring, holier-than-thou, moralistic approach. On the contrary, the values emphasis is energising and excitement-releasing. It challenges members of the organisation to find fun and self-expression in their work.

AN AMERICAN/JAPANESE COMPARISON

From a study which was conceptually linked to Peters and Waterman but completed a little earlier, Pascale and Athos produced *The Art of Japanese Management* (1981). The title is a little misleading because it is primarily a comparative study of two giant modern companies – the Matsushita Electric Company and International Telephone and Telegraph Inc. (ITT).

The two companies are similar on a number of counts. Both are giant international entities. They operate in similar markets and, despite adverse conditions, both were quite successful during the 1970s. They pursued similar business strategies. They operated with 'nearly identical' matrix-type organisational structures. Both relied on formal systems which 'involved detailed planning and financial reports with a highly operational focus' (pp.79–80). 'The real differences lay in the other elements – the management style, the staffing policies and, above all, the spiritual or significant values – and, of course, the human skills to manage all of these' (p.80).

Pascale and Athos make much of the contrasting leadership of Harold Geneen, ITT's chief executive until 1979 and Konosuke Matsushita, founder of the Matsushita Electric Company, who gradually (but not completely) withdrew from a direct management role in the 1970s.

'Harold Geneen has become one important archetype of the successful American manager. He is aggressive, competitive and forceful, downright threatening, hard and decisive. . . Geneen represents, in high relief, a modern version of a historical approach to management. He is Mr Theory X, if you will' (p.151). If Geneen had one primary theme, it was his insistence on 'unshakeable facts' – hard, quantifiable, current data on which decisions could be based. It is interesting to note that in the years leading up to Geneen's retirement several able potential successors were forced out of ITT, and in the years immediately following his retirement the company suffered some serious financial reverses.

Pascale and Athos do not suggest that Mr Matsushita had none of Mr Geneen's tough qualities. Indeed he seems to have exhibited most of them during his long career. However, in addition, Matsushita emphasised and inter-twined into the life of his company a set of values which were specifically religious in origin and very much part of the wider Japanese culture. The seven "spiritual" values of the company (p.51) are:

1 National service through industry.
2 Fairness.
3 Harmony and co-operation.
4 Struggle for betterment.
5 Courtesy and humility.
6 Adjustment and assimilation.
7 Gratitude.

According to Pascale and Athos, Mr Matsushita felt that 'The firm. . . had an inescapable responsibility (which) could best be realised by tying the corporation to society and to the individual by insisting that managers serve as trainers and developers of character, not just as exploiters of human resources' (p.50).

In the Western view such explicit (and frequent) reference to values seems peculiar and some of the accompanying rituals, such as the company song, seem positively laugh-able. There is no suggestion that such rituals could be simply imported. However, there are very practical matters associ-ated with this. As Pascale and Athos point out:

> One can see clearly the great difference between Mr Matsushita and Mr Geneen in the way they "thought" about (and acted towards) people. . . Geneen seemed to regard other people as objects to be used to achieve his purpose, while Matsushita seemed to regard them both as objects to be used and subjects to be honoured in achieving his and their purposes. When Geneen found an executive wanting, the man was humiliated or fired.

When Matsushita made a similar discovery, the man's *group* was marked as ineffective and he was reassigned, even demoted, and the opportunity for the individual to grow from the experience was stressed (p.83).

In addition we may note that, by contrast with Geneen, Matsushita went to great lengths to groom successors and made space for them to take over by moving gradually into retirement (with temporary 'returns' in times of crisis) over a period of years.

As we have noted, there are many senses in which the specifics of Japanese practice are not transferable to the West. However, many observers have been surprised to find how well the Japanese have been able to adapt their techniques of management in Western countries. When Pascale and Athos turned their attention to other Western companies, they found a continuity of theme that had emerged from comparing ITT and Matsushita. They encapsulate the theme in the phrase 'Great companies make meaning', and illustrate this particularly from the experience of IBM, which has always paid particular attention to corporate philosophy and the values inherent in it. As we have seen, the subsequent and linked study by Peters and Waterman has developed these ideas further. Both studies make reference to the dangers of mishandling the development of meaning in companies, and we turn to this subject now.

PITFALLS OF CORPORATE PURPOSE

There are potential dangers inherent in an emphasis on corporate views, superordinate goals, meaning and purpose. The dangers need to be considered, not least because there is evidence to suggest that we are inclined to think 'it couldn't happen here'.

The dangers are essentially those of fanaticism – the release of powerful pent-up energies in destructive causes. Given the history of this century, we have good cause to look cautiously at this subject. Nazism is the most commonly cited example of the power of perverted values driving behaviour. The problem with this example is that it is so large scale that it is easy to ignore the fact that the vast majority of the perpetrators were ordinary people 'just doing their jobs'. They were acting under orders and under the influence of powerful, values-based appeals to their sense of patriotism, duty, comradeship and, indeed, their sense of mission on behalf of humanity.

In this regard – the perpetration of harmful actions in the name of the good – Stanley Milgram's research, published as *Obedience to Authority* (1974), is important, particularly because it deals with the behaviour of large numbers of ordinary people under much less dramatic circumstances than are prevalent during wartime.

The research was conducted at Yale University in the 1960s and later replicated in several other countries. The aim of the experiment was to find out how far people would be obedient when ordered to inflict pain on others in a good cause. The subjects of the experiment (over 1,000 of them at Yale) were volunteers recruited by newspaper advertisements to participate in 'a scientific study of memory and learning'. In this case the values-based 'good' cause was 'Science and Education', personified by the university staff who gave the subjects their instructions.

The subjects were told that they would be testing 'learners' who had also volunteered for the project. The 'subject testers' were told to ask the learners a prearranged set of questions and to punish wrong answers by giving a series of electric shocks. The shocks increased in intensity in accordance with the number of wrong answers given. The 'learners' were out of sight and wired through to a shock generator which had thirty switches marked from 15 to 450 volts. The switches were also marked with signs ranging from 'slight shock' to 'intense shock' to 'danger – severe shock'.

In fact there was no electrical connection and the learners were actually actors trained to answer a certain number of questions wrongly and to simulate responding to shock when the switches were thrown. They had learned a schedule of responses from mild grunts at 75 volts to protests increasing in volume. At 150 volts the learner was to shout that he refused to participate any further. At 315 volts the learner was to let out a loud scream and then fall silent. The 'subject-tester' delivering the shocks, however, had been told to treat silence or failure to answer a question as equivalent to a wrong answer and thus to continue, 15 volts at a time, on up to 450 volts.

If a 'subject-tester' was to object to what he was doing, the professor overseeing him had a set of simple responses from 'Please go on' through 'The experiment requires you to continue' to 'You have no other choice, you must go on'.

Most of us, if asked, would regard as very low the probability of many 'subject-testers' going through with this whole process. Milgram himself and other experts whom he consulted before the experiments thought only a few people would proceed right through the experiment. Indeed many of the people who thought they were giving the shocks did become highly distressed and protested to their white-coated academic supervisors. However, the standard commands ('You must go on', etc.) were sufficient to keep many of them at their voluntary task. In fact, *over 60 per cent completed the experiment*, going right up to the 450-volt mark. Similar or higher proportions of subjects complied with the experiment when it was repeated in Australia, Germany, Italy and South Africa.

We have gone into this example at some length because Milgram's work indicates that behaviour which we would normally term Fascist and/or sadistic is not the preserve of unusual wartime settings. It can be induced in ordinary people by a combination of hierarchical authority and appeal to a higher value – in this case science, a rather familiar and supposedly benign value.

The parallel with corporate life is obvious. There is considerable potential danger in grafting powerful appeals to higher values on to the inbuilt hierarchy of organisations.

THE MEANING PARADOX

Thus, at this stage we are left with a paradox. On the one hand, we have the Japanese experience and the 'excellent' company experience which suggest the virtues of a values–based approach. This appears to be supported by increasing demands from individual employees for more meaning in their work. On the other hand, we know of the excesses that can be generated by the combination of 'values' and hierarchy, and Milgram's work suggests that such excesses can be generated in relatively ordinary settings.

This paradox represents a genuine dilemma, and there is no virtue in pretending that it can be easily dealt with. There is the risk of excess in any attempt to develop and bring alive the value position of an organisation. As with any real dilemma, there is also risk in not making the attempt – the risk that the organisation grows increasingly boring, moribund, aimless and eventually loses the ability to sustain itself.

Evidently there can be no complete safeguards, but the best hope would seem to be that attempts to develop organisational value positions should be firmly grounded in the Western traditions of freedom, self-determination and empiricism. That is to say, there is a need for parallel development of both what the organisation stands for and what its individual members stand for. In this regard Milgram is again instructive. Following the main experiment, he tried a variation in which the 'subject-testers' were given freedom to use any level of shock during the experiment. Under these conditions almost all 'subject-testers' used only the lowest levels of shock available.

Encouraging people to exercise their freedom of choice in a corporate setting may at times be inconvenient and will be uncomfortable for those managers whose self-esteem has come to depend overmuch on their positions. But it is fundamental to a Western style of developing an organisation's value position. It can release much blocked motivation and energy. In addition, it provides a degree of safeguard against excess.

As we suggested earlier, many companies have pockets of

self-developmental, experiential or action learning activity which are a basis for this kind of work. Some organisation development (OD) work has managed to retain its original twin emphasis on values and pragmatism. Our own work with companies in this area in the last several years has centred around the Life Business approach (Eckblad and Bumstead, 1982; Bumstead and Eckblad, 1984).

Charles Handy's writing (1978, 1983) addresses the questions of values and cultures in organisations and individuals. Lancaster University's Centre for Management Learning has specialised in helping managers make sense of and learn from their experience. Sheffield Polytechnic has a particular approach to management self-development (see Pedler *et al.*, 1978). Brunel University's Institute of Organisational and Social Studies runs a series of workshops in self-development. Such issues are much discussed at the recently founded Business Network in London. The list of possible sources of help could be much longer. It is to be hoped that an increasing number of managers will be encouraged to tackle the business of creating meaning – for themselves and their enterprises. We can then begin to bridge and transcend the unhelpful split between meaning and practicality. 'Meaning business' may acquire some new and exciting connotations.

REFERENCES

Bumstead, D. C., 'Paedomorphosis (change through small organisational forms) and the Development of Large Organisations in the Current Crisis', *Management Education and Development*, 14, No.1, 1983.

Bumstead, D. C. and Eckblad, J. P., 'Developing Organisational Cultures', *Leadership and Organisation Development Journal*, 5, No.4, 1984.

Eckblad, J. P. and Bumstead, D. C., 'Managing Your Life Business', *Management Education and Development*, 13, No.1, 1982.

Handy, C., *The Gods of Management*, Pan, 1978. *Taking Stock*, BBC, 1983.

Lessem, R., 'New World of Work', *Industrial and Commercial Training*, October 1982.

Milgram, S., *Obedience to Authority*, Harper & Row, 1974.

Pascale, R. T. and Athos, A. G., *The Art of Japanese Management*, Penguin, 1981.

Pedler, M., Burgoyne, J. G., and Boydell, T. H., *A Manager's Guide to Self Development*, McGraw-Hill, 1978.

Peters, T. J. and Waterman, R. H., *In Search of Excellence*, Harper & Row, 1982.

Robertson, J., *The Sane Alternative*, Robertson, 1983.

6 Intrapreneurship: the way forward?

Sven G Atterhed

The increasing demand by companies for creativity and action on the part of their managers has given rise to the concept of the 'intrapreneur'.

In business today there is a well-developed trend towards decentralisation, causing changes in business operations and philosophy. For example, local managers who suddenly find themselves heading a profit centre will now be forced to think in more business-oriented terms. These new, small profit units are capable of being entrepreneurial and a role has opened up for a special type of manager – increasingly referred to as the 'intrapreneur'. This offers a whole new field of employment.

Traditionally, people have had to choose between being an entrepreneur or an employee if they seek to work in business. Now, the intrapreneurial approach combines the two, bringing many benefits for both the employer and employee. The latent entrepreneur can provide an organisation with the new ideas and projects it especially needs today. This individual is able to implement new concepts and business opportunities which were previously often stifled by rigid organisation. Even if mediocre, an idea supported actively by an entrepreneur is more productive than a good one which dies through the inactivity of an administrator.

Similarly, employees who currently work in a large organisation can have their, so far hidden, business potential tapped and developed by the employer. A large corporation can offer them the extensive back-up service they need, and also provide them with the security of a corporate image.

Certainly figures suggest that there is a wealth of creative talent to draw upon. In 1950, 90,000 entrepreneurs created new firms in the USA. By 1981, this figure had reached over 600,000, an increase of almost seven times. If this creative talent had been harnessed within the corporations, the benefits would have been enormous. Finding, supporting, and encouraging entrepreneurs within the organisation has become essential for the survival of the corporation.

Top management must have a serious commitment to the belief that it must explore totally new areas of opportunity. More substantially, it must be willing to co-operate with these internal entrepreneurs (intrapreneurs) by providing a broad array of financial, technical and personal support, and by treating the scheme realistically, being prepared both for success and failure. The management must also recognise the effects within the corporation if such a change of philosophy is implemented. While it suggests the company is looking for innovaters and risk-takers from within, and that initiative is being encouraged, it may also make some employees feel threatened. Attempts to implement a strong 'intrapreneurship' scheme against the background of a rigid, centralised, hierarchical organisation will fail because the intrapreneurs and the rest of the company will be receiving conflicting signals.

The creation of the intrapreneurship scheme should be seen in the wider context as part of an attempt to stimulate and energise an entire company, like an employment participation scheme. However, it differs in that individual creativity and initiative are stressed and in that it is customer-oriented. It was Gifford Pinchot III, a US management consultant, who created the term 'intrapreneur' to describe these entrepreneurs working within the infrastructure and with the encouragement of the company. The Foresight Group in Sweden put the concept to practical use by setting up the 'School For Intrapreneurs' in 1979, with the idea of screening volunteers from participating companies, then helping the successful applicants to develop their ideas into real business propositions. The process takes several months before the 'intrapreneur' and the company both agree to pursue the venture further. The company acts as a friendly venture capitalist and the individual puts his potential into practice. While both assume some of the positive facets of their counterparts in the external world, neither has to assume the full range of risks.

Rather than just train the intrapreneur, the Foresight Group recognises that the whole company must be prepared for the changed work environment. Planners, for example, are faced with a fresh challenge in having to plan for new, unexpected ventures, to cope with the apparently 'craziest' of intrapreneurs. Such activities must be built into the decision-making process in a way that allows responsible executives to make good judgements about the future well-being of the organisation.

Although it is sometimes difficult to distinguish between eccentricity and originality, the organisation needs to encourage the initiative of individual employees, to give them the atmosphere of freedom to act on opportunities and take on problems. The idea is that this will not apply just to the 2 or 3 per cent of potential intrapreneurs, but rather that the entire organisation will undergo a basic change in mentality – becoming active, thinking and creative.

The fragmented work-style of large organisations has exorcised many individual skills – skills which have to be relearnt. Workers should see their work in the context and perspective of the final object, recognise the part played by their own contribution, and take individual action on this basis. The philosophy behind this viewpoint is that if people feel fully accountable for the course of events, they will develop an entrepreneurial spirit. Figure 6.1 illustrates the changed attitudes of intrapreneurs and those of the company in which they work.

This is not just fanciful idealism, as we can see by the work of the Foresight Group, which, in 1983, after three years of implementing the scheme, came to the following conclusions. Primarily, it is not enough just to create an intrapreneur: it is also necessary to adapt his company to accept him, by telling his colleagues about the concept of intrapreneurship, instilling an atmosphere of co-operation both at top-management and lower down the hierarchy and

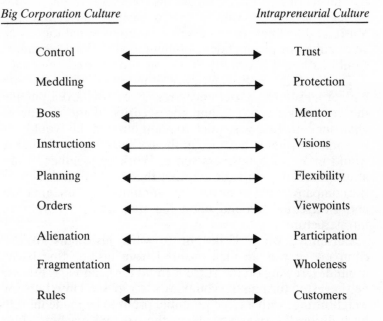

Big Corporation Culture		Intrapreneurial Culture
Control	←——————→	Trust
Meddling	←——————→	Protection
Boss	←——————→	Mentor
Instructions	←——————→	Visions
Planning	←——————→	Flexibility
Orders	←——————→	Viewpoints
Alienation	←——————→	Participation
Fragmentation	←——————→	Wholeness
Rules	←——————→	Customers

Figure 6.1   The corporation and the intrapreneur

establishing a system to recognise potential intrapreneurs. The Group found that there were fewer people than expected within the companies they studied who fitted the standard intrapreneurial pattern. They discovered five major intrapreneurial types, and attached models to them, as follows.

THE GROUNDBREAKING INTRAPRENEUR

Erik, the case model, had been hidden away for years in the information/PR department of Speciality Steel Co. While he was busy informing the customers about the company, the company knew little about Erik. An avid sports fan, he operated a one-man travel agency, organising international visits between soccer teams, and he and a friend had started to market basic sports equipment, such as a soccer marking cone, which he had got a well respected trainer to sponsor, on commission, to minimise the initial expense. These were two facets of Erik hidden from his company. In his private business affairs he wanted to see the job through to the finish, and he knew from personal experience that there was an opening for product development in athletics equipment. Could Erik and Speciality Steel come to an arrangement?

Think of the help Speciality Steel could give: starting budget, research, experience, resources for development, the company's contacts and the security of the corporate environment. Erik was quick to point out that this would not be some charitable gesture on the company's part, rather it would make solid business sense. Working together, in an atmosphere of co-operation rather than hostility and silence, the company could draw on Erik's initiative and imagination and Erik could depend upon the support of a corporate infrastructure.

Certainly, when Erik put forward his plans to the company, it was an idea inspired from his sporting background. Drawing on the current trend for health and fitness, he suggested turning the company's 'scrap' steel into bars for weightlifting, with a large potential profit to be made merely by utilising the overcapacity in the existing machine shop and foundry. All that was needed was the guarded secret of the quality of steel in the bar that the leading competitor used but this could easily be discovered by analysis in the company's metallurgical laboratory and improved on. Erik had shown the company a method of profitable diversification which the company had formerly been blind to – just as they had been to Erik's talents.

The groundbreaking intrapreneur takes his company in a new direction by using slack in its facilities and resources.

THE BRINGHOME INTRAPRENEUR

Carl, the case model, had been recognised in the high-ranking, fast-growing finance company for which he worked as a skilled specialist and good administrator. He was responsible for the data-processing and accounting unit of his company, which was known for financing credit card programmes for large retailers.

In the past the company had contracted out its large debt collection needs to several companies in that field, but Carl recognised the sense and business potential of bringing this activity within the company. It was not just the question of profit, but also of service. Bringing the emotive area of debt collection within the company could ensure that the company's policies, principles and practical recommendations would be followed. All that remained was for Carl to conceptualise his specific idea to reflect the company's image and marketing strategy.

Once he received approval and encouragement, it took Carl only a few weeks to establish a detailed structure, and two weeks after this the new unit sent out its first customer mailing. The new unit, working within the existing accounting section, provided a good, workable, and, most of all, economic solution to the company's debt collection needs.

The 'bringhome' intrapreneur brings into the company services that had previously been bought outside.

THE SPIN-OFF INTRAPRENEUR

Leif, the case model, was in charge of the large machine shop in a corporation, dealing mostly with maintenance but spending about a third of his time installing new equipment. After a series of budget reviews, the unit had been cut back to the point where there were no resources available for investment in the workshop. Leif recognised that the best way out of this dilemma was to expand out of the company and bid on contracts on the open market. While ostensibly a 'yes' man, Leif's faith in his unit inspired him to branch out from internal work to turn a shrinking unit into a profitable asset. He had turned from the defensive to the offensive – from placid acceptance to activity.

To aid his expansion, Leif needed a new NS machine which top management had refused to buy. Leif, therefore, leased one for 6 months, simultaneously signing a contract with one of his first customers to use 60 per cent of the machine's capacity – earning more than the whole rental fee. Top management, once faced with the profitable facts, could only accept the situation – a happy state directly derived from Leif throwing aside his inhibitions and using his skill and initiative to successful ends. Leif's transformation took three years, and he is turning the workshop into a separate company with himself as the majority holder – a direct spin-off. So, a defensive visionary, oblivious to the existence of customers, had been turned into a business-minded, customer-oriented individual.

The typical spin-off intrapreneur brings new life into his unit by breaking away and entering the open market as an independent operator.

THE CORPORATE CULTURE INTRAPRENEUR

Rolf, the case model, headed a service unit dealing with maintenance, transportation, building design, construction and security, and a major problem was assessing the unit's profitability and productivity. Rolf saw the sense in marketing these services both within the company and outside. The unit had many specialised and expensive machines and skilled people. Only through taking on external jobs could the unit survive. Rolf instigated a 'cultural revolution'.

The unit moved from an environment of corporate complacency into an active, aggressive intrapreneurial culture, surveying the field, experimenting, and suggesting ideas to customers. All this exemplifies the idea of 'intrapreneurial leadership', whereby employees can be encouraged by seeing exactly how their efforts may lead to ultimate customer satisfaction.

It was a story of success. Rolf took the initiative to reformulate his unit into a separate subsidiary, whilst introducing the intrapreneurial spirit.

The typical cultural intrapreneur brings about a 'revolution' of this type.

THE PROJECT INTRAPRENEUR

Nils, the case model, was 'sent' to the 'School for Intrapreneurs', unlike the others mentioned previously, who had used that all important capacity, their initiative. Nils, however, seemed to have the potential to be transformed into a creative, self-motivated, businesslike intrapreneur. He was a skilled but ordinary project administrator who began to recognise the sense of seeing a product as a complete concept from beginning to end instead of as an isolated project idea. In practical terms Nils intended to create new products for a new group of customers while using the company's distribution, marketing, pricing and payment system, originally developed for its traditional customers. The task of adaptation would not be easy. Nils adopted an active policy, working out in the field and meeting the customers – becoming customer-oriented. Here we see the basic motive – to ensure that a product development department did not have its enthusiasm and motivation crushed out of it by bureaucracy.

The project intrapreneur transforms himself from a normal project administrator into an intensely business-oriented individual.

So, these are the Foresight Group's five major models based on actual case histories. More cases are reported in *'International Management'*. For example, Rolf Ahlsgren, a shiftworker at AB Iggesunds Bruk pulp and paper mill, came up with the idea of building a 5,000 sq. metre greenhouse with a view to producing 125 tonnes of tomatoes annually. The fuel source of 56,000 cu. metres of bark is provided by Iggesunds as a by-product of their paper mill. Three years later Rolf heads a unit that employs 12 people and grows 150 tonnes of tomatoes a year. The greenhouse is said to be the world's largest for tomato growing. Profits are very healthy after an initial period of usual start-up challenges.

The link between tomatoes and paper may seem at first a little unusual, but how about eels and steel? That's the combination offered by Bengt Jonsson, who established an eel farm in an abandoned 460 cu. metre concrete basin formerly used by Surahammars Bruks AB steel mill, for which he is a draughtsman. The warm water necessary to produce the planned 100 tonnes of eels annually is warmed by waste heat in the company's melting shop. It also has the added advantage that oxygen can be pumped into the basin, to help the eels grow, from the firm's own oxygen plant, which has excess capacity.

Bror Andersson works as a salesman with Forsells Konstess AB, which manufactures prefabricated concrete stairways. Using the company's existing concrete stairway technology, he designed a five-storey precast elevator shaft, for which he received many orders. His success came from listening to his customers' needs. Many had complained to him that to use standard concrete elevator shafts in renovations meant making a hole in the roof. Andersson simply came up with one that could be carried through the front door.

The applicability of Foresight's scheme is diverse, as the list of participating companies shows, ranging from business sectors such as financial services to steel, oil (Exxon), furniture (IKEA), and telecommunications (L.M. Ericsson Group).

The concept of intrapreneurship is being increasingly adopted by giants such as Hewlett-Packard, 3M and IBM. It is also becoming common in medium-sized companies, particularly in the 'sunrise' industries of communications and computer applications, which have deliberately de-centralised to encourage and attract potential intrapreneurs. Another reason for the likely growth of intrapreneurship is the fact that traditional motivators, particularly financial ones, cannot necessarily tempt the intrapreneur to stay, for he will seek to exercise his independence outside the company. Against the background of a predicted shortage of motivated, competent middle management, it seems evident that intrapreneurship will become an essential part of tomorrow's corporations.

7 The enabling company

Ronnie Lessem

Companies are now beginning to emphasise flexibility and are moving away from their formal structure to allow the maximum development of their human resources.

Over the past 200 years industry and society have been radically transformed, particularly in the developed countries. Our life-style, our technology, and the scope of business activity have changed dramatically. Commercial enterprise has evolved from cottage industry to multinational business, spurred on by the revolution in physical and electronic communications. And yet, ironically, our view of business and our theory of the firm have hardly changed at all. There has been just one fundamental change in thinking and behaviour. The shift occurred at the turn of the century, when Frederick Taylor coined the phrase scientific management, in America, and Henri Fayol first wrote about industrial organisation, in France. All the so-called advances in 'management theory', since that time, have been operating under the same invariant premise. The premise is that there are those who manage and these who are managed – employers and employees. Business administration, corporate strategy, operations research, management by objectives (MBO), organisation development, and quality circles have each brought with them a shift in focus, but no fundamental change in business concept. It is only now, in 1984, that a paradigm shift is indeed occurring.

IN THE BEGINNING

Let us start by going back to the beginning, or just before
the Industrial Revolution. In the beginning there was many
a cottage industry, in which domestic and commercial crafts
were unclearly differentiated. Wool was spun for domestic
and for outside consumption on the very same spinning
wheel. Household and economy were closely interwoven, as
were the functions of men and women. Each may have had
its place, but it was side by side.

The Industrial Revolution changed all that, in the same
way as the agrarian revolution had done before it, turning
subsistence agriculture into commercial enterprise. Between
the cottage and industry was placed the technological
entrepreneur. Household and economy were divided, as
were women (who stayed at home) from men (who
performed jobs elsewhere). For the first time we witnessed
employment on a large scale. Until then people had either
been self-employed or else tied to particular sectors of
society, such as the landowners, the royal court or the
military. Employment was a newly emerging phenomenon,
fostered by the entrepreneurs, who required labour, as well
as land and capital for their industrial enterprises. The
cottage and industry become mutually exclusive, in a
productive sense, rather than mutually reinforcing. The
polarity of producer and consumer, employee and house-
holder, replaced the complementarity of cottage – industry.
When the managers took over from the entrepreneurs
nothing changed in one respect, and everything changed in
another.

THE MANAGERIAL REVOLUTION

The managers, who followed their entrepreneurial pre-
decessors, inherited the system of employment. The only
change, though a significant one, was that the emergence of
trade unions transformed individual units of labour into a
collective workforce. But this represented a relative rather
than an absolute change. The employment system remained

undiluted. What did alter was the relation between capital and enterprise. With the advent of the joint-stock company, toward the middle of the nineteenth century, ownership was separated from control. Shareholding became institutionalised. The risk-taking entrepreneur was split between one person who risked his money and another who managed the enterprise. It is this process of managing which has attracted so much attention since then.

Ever since the entrepreneur was removed from real control over his enterprise, a broad set of relationships have emerged to be 'managed'. In other words, activities have had to be deliberately planned for, organised, directed and controlled. The key relationships and functions are set out in Table 7.1.

Table 7.1
The managed organisation

Relationships	Function
Producer and consumer	Marketing
Man and machine	Production
Manager and worker	Personnel
Shareholder and manager	Finance
Commerce and technology	Research and development
Business and environment	Business policy

These particular relationships resulted from a method of organising business and society that separated producer from consumer, man from machine, manager from worker, commerce from technolgoy, and business from environment. They needed to be understood and effectively handled if the managed organisation was to survive and prosper. All the management theories, analytical and behavioural, mechanistic and organic, operational and strategic, have operated under this basic premise.

PARADIGM SHIFT

We are now witnessing, for the first time in almost 100 years, a fundamental paradigm shift. This shift is occurring under the parallel and interrelated influence of technology, psychology, and economics. It is creating a new force out of an old set of relationships.

Technologically, we have entered an age of miniaturisation, as managed organisations are being turned into distributed networks. Psychologically, we have entered an era of personalised life-styles, where rigid family and business structures are being turned into flexible and interdependent entities. Economically, we have entered a phase of decentralisation. Centralised organisations are being turned into profit centres and autonomous divisions, evolving into not only the old orthodoxy, but also into a spate of joint ventures, management buy-outs, subcontracting and personal networking that is unprecedented. Whereas the move from functional organisations to profit centres or project management represented an evolutionary change, the move towards all kinds of contemporary joint ventures is a revolutionary one. Why then is this so? What is the fundamental discontinuity with which we are faced, and what are its implications? To answer these questions we need, once more, to retrace our steps.

The creation of the limited liability company in the nineteenth century separated the person from the business, establishing an independent identity. As such, the public company could stand on its own two feet, existing separately from its shareholders, consumers and employees. It competed freely in the market place, and asserted its independent identity by securing market share and acquiring profits. As a logical extension of such competitive and expansive activity, many such enterprises turned into holding companies. In other words, by acquiring other companies, which may have previously been competitors, they strengthened their scope and competitive advantage. They acquired as a result not only more physical and financial assets, but more people as employees. The Standard Oils, the General Motors, the IBMs were and are very good examples of such holding companies. What they hold is the company man, as well as the company plant and the company car. The urge to acquire and to possess, to compete and to conquer, was all-embracing. If they failed to compete successfully, they would lose their hold on their people and their assets, and subsequently lose control. It is almost as if they had to hold on, for dear life, to their subjects' identity.

Of course, for some years now, the holding company has been losing control. Company man, though still alive and well in some circles, is no longer in general fashion. Labour-intensive industries, which held on to thousands of people, are losing out to their more automated counterparts. Machines are today more willingly possessed than people. E.F. Schumacher did the controlling mentality no favour when he declared so persuasively that 'Small is Beautiful'. Steve Jobs deliberately set out to give power to the small business people when he started his microcomputing revolution, with more than a taste of Apple. Sinclair made us sit up and think when he created a £27 million manufacturing business by employing forty-nine people, and sub-contracting the bulk of the routine work out to Timex. Then there was 'F' (for flexible) International, one of the biggest software and systems house in the land, employing or really deploying women from their homes. Something significant was afoot. The fact that hundreds of journalists devoured like hungry lions the news of Rank Xerox's 'Networking' scheme was no accident. After all, did a few people working on a new sub-contract basis give us so much to shout about? In 1976, Norman Macrae's extremely thought-provoking article on the Entrepreneurial Revolution, in comparison, hardly gained any notice. The time, of course, in 1983 (but not 1976) was right. The paradigm is now shifting.

To amuse myself I keep regular score of the many articles that now appear in the *Financial Times* on joint ventures of one kind or another being formed. I include a sample of these in Table 7.2. What, then, is it all about? Has the concept of the public company, and its logical extension, the holding company, been eclipsed? The answer must be that it has not been eclipsed, for the seeds of revolution are not sown right across the land for all to see. After all, when the first microcomputers were on the horizon they were hardly spotted, and technological change is much faster than social and economic transformation.

Table 7.2
Joint ventures

Collaborators	Mode	Description
Rolls Royce–General Electric (USA)	Risks revenue-sharing	The two major companies are to become partners in the development and manufacture of two high-power aircraft engines, one from each.
Thorn EMI–Virgin Records	Fostering competitors	The majors have every reason to foster their smaller competitors because they need to *fill spare capacity*, by selling their services to them.
Pitney Bowes–small business	Piggy-backing	The company has recently launched a search for innovative products to distribute through its nationwide marketing and service network, *aimed at companies* with good office system products and *limited means of marketing* them.
Lewis Brothers–Remploy	Shared production	Under a new £3.5 million contract, Remploy will make choc ices for Lewis Brothers. The arrangement will *enable Lewis* to make *more ice-cream,* without new investment in a building.
Ford–Uruguay/Levi-Strauss–Hungary/Pierre Cardin–China	Barter	Ford *trades* its cars for thousands of Uruguayan sheepskins; Levi–Strauss sells a turnkey plant to Hungary, and gets jeans in return; Pierre Cardin gets oriental skills by providing consultancy services to China.
Acorn–Fledgling high tech enterprises	Venture capital	Acorn wants to help companies in technical areas regarded as promising. These companies often find difficulty in getting cash from conventional sources.
Barclays–de Zoete and Bevan–Wedd Durlacher	Arranging links	Barclays has arranged links with a stockbroker and a jobber to form the core and basis for development of a powerful new international securities company.

The holding company has not been eclipsed, rather a rival has come up in its midst. That rival I shall call the enabling company. Whilst the role of the enabler has been visible in the training world for years, the enabling company is something else. Whereas the enabler develops people's potential, the enabling company develops the potential of markets, technology, production plants and corporate finance, as well as the potential of people. Moreover, and this is the key, enabling involves not holding down but holding together, not employing but deploying, not competing but co-operating, not overpowering but empowering people, technology, customers, and whole companies.

The means to that end, as revealed in Table 7.2, ranges from piggy-backing, to 'production sharing', from barter to risk and revenue sharing, from partnerships and alliances to networks and linking arrangements. Whereas the managerial revolution created a breed of manager who supplanted the entrepreneur, the networking revolution is creating a breed of enabler who can both accommodate and supersede the manager and entrepreneur. In other words, entrepreneurial transactions and managed structures exist within an overriding and enabling network. As a result potential is not only exploited (entrepreneur) and channelled (manager), but also developed. Exploitation is based on dominance and acquisition, and channelling upon structure and control. Development is based upon understanding and transmitting the forces of evolution and the interdependent features in man and machine, company and environment.

THE ENABLING COMPANY

Mature companies should not be attempting to develop 'enterprising organisations'. That would be going back a step, rather than forwards. Those of us who call for entrepreneurial managers have our hearts in the right place, but not our heads. What we should be creating instead are enabling organisations, which contain within them, but are not constrained by, managed structures and entrepreneurial transactions (Figure 7.1).

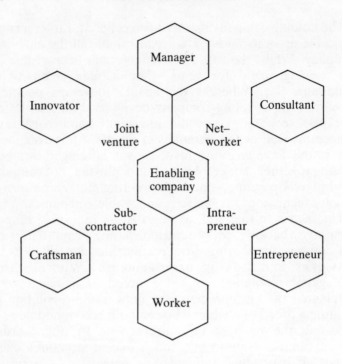

Figure 7.1 The enabling company

I would propose a triangular framework that companies could adopt. I notice, in fact, that 'F' International is organised very much along the lines of Figure 7.2. Whereas the managing director would be responsible for the channelling of already recognised products, market and human potential, the development director would operate quite differently. He or she would be orchestrating the development of entrepreneurial, networking, and joint venture potential that does not lend itself to formal organisation or to manager-employee relations. The very terms 'enabler', 'entrepreneur' and 'networker' fall outside bounded organisational constraints. The direction of development is evolutionary, unpredictable, discontinuous, and interactive.

Retrospectively a pattern will emerge, but not prospectively. That is why the distributed network is much more amenable to such a configuration than the centralised

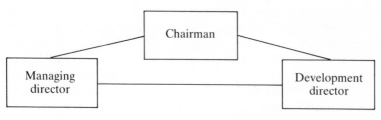

Figure 7.2

organisation. Ultimately, it is for the chairman, the nucleus of the organisation, to explode the dilemma of left versus right, to transform any serious conflict into creative tension. At the stage when this creativity activity moves to the leading edge, we shall move even beyond the enabling company.

Enabling organisations will contain both employees and what might be called 'imployees'. Conventional managers and workers constitute the employees. As indicated in Figure 7.1, they are employed directly by the company. However, a growing number of people will become detached imployees, who are only indirectly or partially 'employed'. Consultant networkers, as evidenced by 'F' International and Rank Xerox, have already become a well known form of 'imployee'. They provide an independent service to the company, as only part of their business activity. The most likely candidates for networking include training and PR, financial and investment analysts. All branches of computer-based 'intrapreneurs', although functioning within the company, are liable to be offered considerable freedom and autonomy, and may also share in the profits of their venture. In a true enabling company they will have additional scope to develop their own completely independent business, as long as it does not divert their efforts unduly. Unlike the networker, who is self-employed but not necessarily of entrepreneurial bent, the 'intrapreneur' is a genuine 'wheeler-dealer'. The craftsman or tradesman, operating as a closely connected sub-contractor, may or may not be entrepreneurial in his approach, but he too will retain his independent status, and take over – as Norman Macrae suggested as long ago as 1976

– an increasing number of activities that are peripheral to the company's core business. Prime candidates are travel and secretarial services, maintenance work and road transport, printing and distribution, office cleaning and catering. Finally, there are the proliferating joint ventures, many of which are associated with innovation and new product development. The innovator fits much more comfortably into a footloose relationship than as an employee within the firm.

Interestingly enough, the most progressive chairmen, such as Steve Shirley, John Harvey Jones and Sir Adrian Cadbury, perform very much of the enabling function. The problem is that, because we have not acknowledged and accelerated the paradigm shift, the managed orthodoxy conceals the enabling activity at the top. This is because there are several layers of organisation and activity, and the one that symbolises our paradigm shift is least visible. Physical activity is there for all to see in the shape of plant, machinery and manual work. Social arrangements are reflected in the restaurant, the pub, the company news-paper, and sporting or leisure facilities. Information process-ing is visible both in the form of letters and reports, and also increasingly in disks and data banks. Entrepreneurial activity, although not as prevalent in large organisations as in small, is symbolised by product champions, wheeler-dealers, artful negotiations, aggressive salespeople, and financial incentive systems. The formal organisation chart is there for all to see, including job descriptions, lines of command, grading structures, and administrative rules and procedures. Each of these has its place, but no longer at the leading edge. It is the invisible enabling function, which is just beginning to show its face through the alliances, networks, linkages and co-operative arrangements brought about by joint ventures, that now needs to gain force.

In summary, then, the enabling company 'enables' entre-preneurs, craftsmen, innovators and networkers (and some-times even managers, in the context of a 'buy-out' or franchise) to fulfil their individual potential and, in the process, to realise the company's business potential. Each and every one of these 'imployees' is operating in a way that is not only quite different from conventional employment, but also different from each other. That is a situation that the enabling organisation, unlike the conventional holding company, accommodates.

8 Flexible working years

Bernard Teriet

Radical changes are also happening with work times. The recent development of the flexi-year concept has proved to be successful in many German firms.

The reduction of the working week from 40 hours may currently be the top priority of trade unions and other pressure groups in Europe, but it is only one of a range of interesting approaches aimed at overcoming the rigidity of working patterns. One of the most far-reaching experiments concerns the working-year contract, or the flexible working year. This alters several of the basic tenets of working times. For a start, it uses the year, instead of the week or month, as the reference period against which working times are measured. This means that working hours for the first time come into line with every other important planning cycle within the organisation.

Conventionally, weekly hours are, for most companies, the basis of all their working-time arrangements. The relevance and usefulness of using this short time frame is now becoming questionable, since, in a business economy, most references are yearly. It makes better economic sense to adopt a flexible working-year arrangement, and fit working times to people's individual time needs, while simultaneously evening out fluctuations in working times over a much broader reference period.

The flexi-year system is put into operation through a working-time contract which is agreed between employer and employee. The net working hours of the employee during one whole year are decided, and from then on the employee is largely free to choose his or her working times. He or she is obliged to fulfil his or her yearly quota, yet is able to enjoy a high degree of freedom and flexibility. Often a supervisor may be appointed to an employee, in order to co-ordinate as closely as possible the interests of the company with the wishes of the employee. Under the scheme employees can choose at 6-monthly intervals (or less) to reassess the number of hours they wish to work, and, if necessary, decrease or increase their quota. The scheme allows for both flexibility and a high degree of precision planning.

Once initiated, the flexi-year benefits both the employee and the company. Most importantly, the scheme offers enormous potential in increased flexibility for the two parties. The scheme has the following advantages for the employee:

1 The working-year model can be an umbrella under which he or she can expect a maximum of working time flexibility, whilst also being offered multiple alternative work patterns. The alternative work patterns may be on a weekly basis, such as the flexi-day, or based on larger monthly variations.
2 It maintains a secure and regular system of payment, since he or she is paid a regular monthly salary, regardless of how many hours worked during that period.

The employer has the following advantages:

1 An improved ability to handle seasonal or cyclical fluctuations in productions and sales during the year.
2 Better opportunities to avoid alternations between over-time and short-time periods by synchronising working hours and business hours according to the imperative of the market.
3 The chance to hire and employ an optimal workforce made up of full-timers and part-timers who have a high potential of flexibility.
4 Fitting working times to people's individual time-needs encourages them to respond with greater productivity, lower absenteeism and lower labour turnover.

5 It allows the company to take full advantage of the vast
   pool of part-time labour and other non-standard arrangements such as job-sharing, seasonal working and tandem
   jobs.

Despite these advantages, companies have been surprisingly
slow to adopt the flexi-year arrangement. For the last 10
years several individuals and prestigious bodies have been
advocating the scheme. The president of the Volvo plant in
Sweden urged, in 1976, the abolition of the 8-hour day, by
arguing that individuals have enough maturity and responsibility to decide for themselves their own rhythm of life and
ideal work input. This could be achieved through a contract
between employee and employer. The French confederation
of employees, in the second half of the 1970s, also proposed
the use of the working-year contract as the basis of
reorganising the French working-hours system. In addition,
for the last 20 years, many West German companies have
been seriously considering new work arrangements and have
been interested in further advancements of the flexi-time
concept. The scheme has been introduced in a variety of
ways in West Germany, and it is interesting to see how this
has been achieved and the exact conditions of the scheme.

   The flexi-year scheme was implemented on a small scale in
several German firms, who used it to cater for certain
employees who wanted specific flexible working patterns
which could not be realised under the conventional part-
time scheme. The employer had the choice of either losing a
useful employee or finding a solution to the problem. Under
these circumstances, the flexi-year became a new basis for
co-operation between the company and the employee.
However, this approach had a high degree of exclusiveness,
and rigid working patterns continued to exist for the rest of
the firm. These cases could not be used as precedents since
they were contracted in this limited and semi-private
manner.

   However, the flexi-year arrangement has been used in
firms for the whole staff and the two cases may be examined.
The first is the case of Kaufhaus Beck, a retail store in
Munich. The company wished to improve customer service

while providing more flexibility in working hours for the staff. For the former objective, the company analysed the number of customers dealt with in each day of the week. This analysis became the basis for their manpower planning. For the latter objective, the company analysed the desired working patterns of the staff. At the end of the analysis the company designed a scheme for working periods on the basis of monthly hours. Staff were given different options for time periods, ranging from 60 hours per month to 173 hours per month. The employee was presented with flexible alternative work patterns, while the employer had the opportunity to build up an optimal work force with built-in flexibility, improving conditions not only for the staff but also for the customer. This arrangement has been working successfully since July 1978.

The second company installed seven different options for its employees, ranging from over 90 per cent to under 40 per cent of the normal working year. The company used the flexi-year concept as the umbrella for the different categories of staff, such as full-timers, part-timers and temporary helpers. Under this umbrella, full-timers have obtained the opportunity to work less than 40 hours without losing their full-time status. The spectrum of part-time work could also be widened. Most importantly, a fundamental change in temporary employee's status took place, since they were able to become permanent employees of the company. They were an invaluable group who were ready to work for the company whenever needed.

Implementing the scheme on a more widespread basis into whole industries and large firms is the next step. Although not yet achieved, it will be by no means impossible to introduce the scheme into West Germany in the next few years. Two important events have had a bearing on the scheme's increased popularity. The first is the project of the German Volkswagen AG, which is employing the flexi-year as a new basis for its organisation. It is clear that such a move would be more than a pilot project in the country – certainly it would act as a signal to other German automobile producers and their subsidiaries. The second significant event occurred in the recent tariff agreements on new work and business hours regulations. This was based on the normal 38.5-hour week, but allowed for this average to be reached through different strategies. Taking effect from the spring of 1985, these new regulations will encourage the idea and practice of alternative work patterns. Employers' associations and trade unions will soon have to learn to live with these new modes of working hours.

The attitude of the government is also an important factor towards the successful implementation of the flexi-year on a large scale in West Germany. Although the present government does not actively support the concept, it is encouraging that it does not erect legal and administrative barriers for both employees and employers. However, several strategies are needed to assist the introduction of the flexi-year, and since the change is inevitably taking place, the government should assist this process and employ its own considerable administrative and operational powers. Other important factors necessary for the more widespread use of the flexi-year are:

1 A widening of the general consciousness of the business world, so that it realises working flexibility is a concept here to stay. Managers now need to think of time as one of the key resources they manage, and learn to design more optimal solutions in this field.

2 The flexi-year must no longer be introduced into individual companies in such a segmented, unplanned way. The concept must now be handled in a deliberate, organised manner, with both the employer and employee thoroughly researching the possibilities of alternative work patterns within the flexi-year.

3 The economics of new work patterns must also develop further. Increased research into this field needs to be undertaken, and more specific background knowledge needs to be acquired, together with more guidelines about implementation.

4 Lastly, a continual feedback between research and actual situations must be established, so that experiments may be properly evaluated, and research may adequately keep up with current developments.

It is clear that the flexi-year concept as one model of alternative working patterns is no longer merely an ideal. Many firms, particularly in the Republic of Germany, are recognising the unique opportunities and benefits which the flexi-year offers to both the employer and employee. Implementation is still slow and cautious, and lacks organisation particularly, but the concept has now definitely become a reality, and in recent years the tempo of its penetration has increased.

9 Sabbaticals: the John Lewis experience

Stephen May

Alternative work patterns may even include 6-month sabbaticals. The John Lewis pilot scheme reveals the advantages and disadvantages of such a scheme.

The long leave scheme operated by the John Lewis Partnership department stores and Waitrose supermarkets group is one of the many ways in which profits are shared among all the 26,000 people who work in the business and are its beneficial owners. This scheme commemorates a significant date in the Partnership's history, giving life to a concept first expressed by the Founder, John Spedan Lewis, in 1954.

The date it commemorates is that of the First Trust Settlement in 1929, by which Spedan Lewis began the long process of transferring his rights in the retail business he had just inherited to those working in it, present and future. At that time it comprised two London department stores, John Lewis in Oxford Street and Peter Jones in Sloane Square.

Fifty years later his nephew, Peter Lewis, who is now the Partnership's third Chairman, was considering a fitting way of celebrating this event. Among the possibilities was an idea mooted by Spedan Lewis as early as 1954, shortly after the Partnership had been fully established by means of a Second Settlement in Trust. He had felt that when the Partnership became more prosperous, some kind of sabbatical would be 'a very good thing' so that Partners 'could plan to do things that they would enjoy extremely and that otherwise would not be possible'.

In December 1978, therefore, to mark the anniversary,

Peter Lewis proposed that the Partnership should offer to Partners (as all employees are called) of 25 years' membership, and who had reached the age of 50, a period of up to 6 months' fully paid long leave.

After discussion in the Partnership's various Branch Councils and Central Council (bodies of elected and ex officio representatives which meet regularly to debate and make recommendations concerning the Partnership's affairs) and through the correspondence columns of the weekly house journal, *The Gazette,* the proposal was accepted. It was implemented in April 1979 with a proviso that arrangements might be reviewed in the light of several years' experience.

In 1983, with the experience of long leave enjoyed by nearly 600 Partners to draw on, I carried out a full review of the long leave scheme: its operation, its benefits, its repercussions on the business and individual problems. I concluded that long leave had entirely lived up to its purpose and that few changes were needed.

INTRODUCTION OF THE SCHEME

The scheme, as put forward by the Chairman, provided those who had completed 25 years' membership and had reached the age of 50 with a period of fully paid leave. This was calculated on a formula of one week's leave for every full year of membership completed before the age of 50, the leave to be taken in one consecutive period. In the drafting of detailed rules for the scheme it was agreed there would be a maximum entitlement of 26 weeks.

It was recognised that some special provision would have to be made for those already over 50 when the scheme was introduced. This was made by scaling down the entitlement of people in this category, according to age, although the management's original proposals were improved at the behest of the Central Council. The principle that the nearer the Partner was to retirement age the shorter would be the leave was retained, but with a minimum of ten weeks.

While the entitlement of those already qualified at the

time of the scheme's introduction created a larger number taking long leave initially, now there are just over 100 Partners who become eligible every year – about 1 in 200, or four or five people in an average sized department store. The total cost of providing for such absence cannot be calculated precisely because it depends upon individual circumstances, whether additional resources have to be provided or whether the work is covered by deputies or other members of the department in question. The 1984 value of the original approximation would be about £300,000 a year.

In putting forward the scheme the Chairman said: 'The argument for something of this kind is that it would make for a fuller life for those entitled to the benefit. The opportunity to withdraw for a while from everyday employment, without financial disadvantage and with the assurance of return to the same job, is something that only the employer can give. It cannot be earned, or acquired, or saved, or created, in any other way by the Partner on his own initiative'. He made it clear that he would not wish the scheme to be introduced without the whole-hearted support of the Central Council. 'I should want in particular to see whether the Council gave its support to discrimination in favour of long service Partners and felt that the Partnership as a whole in the future would sustain that privilege without regret or anomalies'.

Amid vigorous correspondence in *The Gazette* on the subject, I published, in January 1979, a list of all the questions I expected would be asked about long leave arrangements, together with answers in order to clarify the proposals before the Central Council. That February the Council was virtually unanimous in welcoming the proposals in principle. Two months later I introduced detailed rules for the scheme, which were accepted by the Central Council in May.

SOME IMPORTANT ARRANGEMENTS

Pay. Partners on leave would receive their basic contractual pay plus an adjustment if overtime pay formed a regular and substantial part of their earnings.

Key jobs. Partners doing specialist or senior management jobs were not to feel indispensable. They were to give 12 months' notice (6 months for other Partners) and arrangements would be made to cover their absence by (i) an attachment for a trainee, (ii) reorganisation of colleagues' responsibilities to share out work. An advantage emerging from this would be that other Partners would have an opportunity to take a higher level of responsibility – on-the-job career development could be a valuable broadening of experience.

Return. Partners would return to the same job unless they requested a change.

Timing. Every effort would be made to enable Partners to choose their own timing for the break, although management would have the final discretion.

Financial assistance. When accepting the new rules in May 1979, the Central Council voted to set aside an extra sum of money for grants to Partners to enable them 'to make fuller use than would otherwise be possible of opportunities afforded to them by long leave'. This was in accord with the Partnership's practice for many years of providing funds for people to pursue their interests. It was hoped that people might make imaginative use of their leave by, for example, visiting relations on the other side of the world or undertaking a period of full-time study, but there was no obligation on Partners to do anything in particular.

USE OF LONG LEAVE

In reviewing the benefits felt by those taking long leave in these early years, I found a wide variety of profitable experience. For some there was the opportunity to pursue a project, or hobby, continuously rather than in their spare time. I heard regular references to an improvement in the quality of life and experience. Some attended art courses. Others took up charitable works. In one case the time was used to build a house extension, and, not surprisingly, there was a great deal of travel. It had come to be regarded as 'a chance in a life time' and the local house magazines carried examples of the impressively wide range of undertakings by at least a substantial minority.

One man, whose hobby had been to keep boa constrictors in his drawing room, was able to do voluntary work in the reptile house at London Zoo; another cycled around France with his wife; a keen amateur photographer took his camera into the Andes; a lady from Peter Jones went trekking in the Himalayas, which she found 'not too strenuous after having been on her feet all day for years'; and a husband and wife team spent 4½ months touring Europe 'like gypsies' in a caravan. They visited nine countries, covering 6,000 miles, and want to do the same again when they retire.

There is no sign of an adverse reaction to this privilege for a minority from colleagues who do not qualify for it. Perhaps some have an eye to the future but, more generally, it is viewed with some pride as an addition to the business' character. It is certainly a talking point for those who have no entitlement themselves but who have readily and willingly accepted the added burden created by absence.

Issues that arose in the course of the review included an apparent difficulty for a minority in settling back into the work routine. To the extent that the relatively few people so affected were largely in the older age groups (with leave taken under the introductory arrangements), it may be a short-term effect. Nevertheless, a lot happens in a retail business in 6 months and some thought has been given to easing the process of re-entry so that, now, some kind of introductory programme is arranged in every case.

Not surprisingly holders of senior posts have found it most difficult to get away on long leave, and this problem has not yet been fully resolved. But the Partnership has remained true to the principle of accepting some disadvantage to its business in exchange for a benefit of real significance for those who remain within it for perhaps their entire working life. So even those in key positions are encouraged to accept that long leave should be possible and worthwhile.

To the arrangements for financial assistance already made by the Central Council has been added some guidance on saving, in the form of an advisory leaflet, which is issued to those within 5 years of qualifying for long leave.

Potentially the most far-reaching of the changes considered by the Personnel Department is the possible reduction in the qualifying age from 50 to 45. It was pointed out from several quarters, in the course of the review, that this would be more truly a mid-career break, and that perhaps those concerned would receive more stimulus from their leave, and return less vulnerable, if it could be taken a little earlier. Because the Partnership is in the process of learning to cope, in 1984, with an additional (fifth) week's holiday for those with over 3 years' service, it has been accepted that it would be premature simultaneously to increase the numbers entitled to long leave. However, the intention is to consider at the end of the year a progressive reduction in the qualifying age, from 49 to 45 over a 5-year period.

Among a number of minor changes to the rules, following the review, perhaps the most significant is one providing that those who qualify within 5 years of retirement may be required to take long leave immediately before their departure. The reason for this is that long leave taken within a few years of retirement cannot be a real mid-career break, so the disruption to the Partnership's efficiency is less justified. Initially I also proposed changing the rule which allows two separate periods of service with the Partnership to be amalgamated in calculating entitlement and recommended that service would have to be continuous, since those who left the company, in effect, were giving themselves a break. The Central Council, however, argued strongly against such a change and their wishes have been allowed to prevail.

10 Job sharing

Pam Walton

Job sharing has social and economic consequences for society, and can offer individuals a unique chance to change the structure of their own lives fundamentally.

Full-time work does not suit everyone, and job sharing is a way of opening up jobs that have previously only been available on a full-time basis to those who need to work fewer hours.

In theory this means that all jobs can be considered available on a full-time or job-sharing basis. As one employer put it, 'Never assume that job sharing cannot take place; look at each job and its component parts before making that decision'.

Job sharing is not the same as job splitting. The government's Job Splitting Scheme was introduced in January 1983, with a £338,500 advertising campaign. Under the scheme, employers receive a £750 grant for every job split. When the scheme was announced, it was condemned by the TUC, the Equal Opportunities Commission, and New Ways to Work (formerly the Job Sharing Project), the national group promoting job sharing in the UK. The main argument against the scheme from all these groups was that whereas job sharing aims to open up reasonable jobs for those who wish to work part-time, job splitting is aimed at people who want and are able to work full-time but who cannot find a job. It is restricted to those unemployed and receiving benefit, or under a redundancy notice. However, the scheme has not been a success, and even after some small modifications were made in the summer of 1983, take-up has continued to be slow. By the end of November 1984 only 990 jobs had been split, although allowance had initially been made for splitting at least 50,000 jobs.

Both in this country and in the USA job sharing was initially used mainly by women who saw that it opened up possibilities of continuing in reasonable paid work while bringing up children. It has continued to be used as a way of enabling women and men who want to combine paid work with childcare to do so. Increasingly women who take maternity leave but do not want to return on a full-time basis are successfully negotiating to return on a job-shared basis.

The recent ruling of an Employment Appeal Tribunal (June 1984), which decided that the Home Office unlawfully discriminated against a full-time woman civil servant on the ground of her sex, by refusing to allow her to work part-time after the birth of her child, will significantly improve this group's bargaining power. A survey carried out by one city council of female employees who had left their employment for maternity reasons found that, out of forty women, thirty-three would be looking to return to work on a part-time basis. This council is now to consider a job-sharing scheme. Men are continuing to negotiate job sharing for similar reasons: 'to spend more time with my daughter and share home responsibilities', and to have 'an opportunity to attempt total equality in a marriage . . . a kind of family life without sex-defined roles at home or at work'.

Some parents even manage to share the same job and childcare. New Ways to Work currently has details of twelve such couples, and, as one of these noted, 'it is more economical than one person leaving work completely', as each person would be eligible for a tax allowance. Single parents may benefit too, as long as the full-time wage is high enough. As one single parent commented, although she found it a struggle to manage on the income, she felt it would be detrimental to her daughter if she worked full-time. For many women who have already left paid jobs for childcare and other domestic reasons job sharing can ease the transition back into the job market after years at home.

Job sharing can also be a creative and positive way in which people with disabilities can work to their full

potential. Not all of them want to be typists, telepho₁
gardeners, traditional jobs found for people with disat
In January 1984 Leeds City Council considered a re₁
job sharing which suggested that full-time work
sometimes be too strenuous for people with disabili₁
recommended job sharing as an important equal op₁
ties measure. It can equally benefit those (usually ₁
who look after chronically sick, disabled and elderly
at home.

Job sharing may be appropriate to people who have o₁
interests they want to pursue and 'want to lead a more vari₁
and balanced life'; and for one sharer it was 'a conscious
decision to opt for a lower material standard of living – time
is more valuable than money'. To some, job sharing can
provide the opportunity to study, like the person on a
part-time librarianship course who shares a job in a library.
For those with artistic interests a shared job can give them
time for their own work, while providing them with a basic
wage. Two brothers share a job as picture framer at a gallery
in Norfolk on an alternate week basis, and in their week 'off'
work on their own paintings. There are also a number of
musicians who want to share jobs for similar reasons.

In the USA the use of job sharing as a way of easing into
retirement is more widespread than in the UK, and a
number of companies offer workers this option. An American insurance company, Travellers, redesigned its pension
policy to allow retired employees to work up to 960 hours
per year while receiving a full pension, and then began to
offer a number of part-time options, including job sharing,
to older workers and retirees.

In the UK, pensions are the main stumbling block, as the
current inflexibility of many occupational schemes can
create problems for job sharers. Where an employee is a
member of a scheme which calculates the pension according
to final salary, job sharing as a way of easing into retirement
could radically affect the amount of pension payable. In an
attempt to encourage workers nearing retirement to share
their jobs with unemployed people the government introduced the Part Time Job Release Scheme in March 1983. In
addition to the half wage received from the employer, the

individual received a small taxable allowance. However, the scheme has a similar limitation to that of the job-splitting scheme, in that the new sharer must be recruited from those receiving supplementary or unemployment benefit.

To a large extent job sharing has been initiated by individuals who have been working full-time and have persuaded their employer to let them job share. If the employer does not want to lose a valued employee, they may be in a strong position to negotiate. As one employer put it, 'I became interested in the idea when I saw how many women – who had very good qualifications and who had been with us a while and whom we had trained – were leaving because they could not cope with both full-time work and family. It seemed an awful waste'. One fear that employers do voice is that they will not be able to find a suitable 'other half'. Experience so far indicates that this is not usually a problem, and even in a small Welsh town an advertisement for a job-sharing librarian brought in twenty-two applicants. However, it is a potential problem with a highly specialised job in a sparsely populated area.

Another way of seeking a shared job is for two people to get together and apply jointly for a job. Some have been successful with this approach, even where an employer has not previously considered the idea, if they have together proved to be the best 'person' for the job. Where someone is unable to find a partner to apply with, it is still worth applying alone. One voluntary organisation in London did appoint a woman on this basis, and then advertised for the other half. However, success is likely to be limited unless the applicant is offering exactly what the employer is looking for. Another approach to looking for a shared job is to do what two women in South London did a few years ago – apply jointly to an employment agency. For some people who are working together already for the same employer, finding a partner may not be a problem, as was the case for two librarians working in London who 'met on a working party, and as we were both pregnant at approximately the same time we considered a job share, and then when we'd prepared a case asked our employers, who said yes'.

For others the task will be harder. One way is to advertise

in a newspaper or specialist journal. The *Library Association Journal* even has a job-sharing column in its vacancies section. In some areas specialised registers have been set up. There is currently one for doctors run by the British Medical Association, and a number for planners run by regional branches of the Royal Town Planning Institute. Another for librarians is run by the Women in Libraries group. A computerised Job Sharing Partner Service is run by NWW for the Greater London area, and Sheffield also has a register.

Mary Kidston and Shirley Karat were one such couple who met through the NWW register in 1982. Mary, a qualified town planner with 10 years' experience, but who was out of work when she registered with NWW, was contacted by Shirley, also a qualified town planner, who had continued to work on a freelance basis for the consultancy firm she had been with for 2 years following the birth of her daughter. However, the work was erratic and she was paid on a part-time hourly rate. Wishing to get her hours on a regular footing and seeing Mary's details on the register, Shirley wrote to her; they met and found they got on well. They then started looking for any jobs in their field which they could apply for together. They met frequently and discussed how they would sell themselves as job-sharers to an employer. They sent two curricula vitae and a joint covering letter with each application. They stress the importance of making out a convincing case to prospective employers: 'You've got to be serious about working out the application, and get across the point about being able to offer a wide range of experience'.

Eventually their hard work paid off. After ten letters and three interviews they were offered a 1-year contract job with the Royal Town Planning Institute's Planning Aid for Londoners. It was a success, their employers were happy, and when the contract was almost up they applied together for another job. This was as a Senior Planning Officer for the London Borough of Camden, which already had a job-sharing policy. They were again successful and they now work alternate days for Camden, both working together on a Wednesday to give continuity. (Other ways of sharing may include dividing the day, dividing the week, working alternate weeks, or even alternate 6-monthly periods. Where it is not necessary to provide total office cover, sharers may work the same 2½ days.) Mary and Shirley feel that they have a lot to offer, and get on extremely well together. Looking at their long-term prospects, they are aware that it is important for employers to recognise that job sharers can take positions of responsibility, and would consider them for promotion. Mary and Shirley themselves applied jointly for internal vacancies three months after arriving at Camden. They were delighted to find that Camden was not only prepared to employ job-sharers but to allow their careers to develop and take on management responsibility. The department recognised them as a well integrated double act, offering good value for money, and promoted them to project officer on a principal officer grade.

The issue of promotion for job sharers is an important one. Given that in the UK and even more so in USA senior and supervisory jobs are successfully shared, there seems to be no good reason why sharers should not be jointly considered for promotion. The question of whether sharers can successfully supervise others is often asked, and it is important to be aware of the danger of job sharers being 'played off' against each other. In addition, it is essential to have the procedure for dealing with problems with members of staff well worked out – this is good management practice anyway. The Head of Personnel at the Stock Exchange, where they have recently upgraded a set of job sharers from Senior Training Officer to Training Manager, also comments that these days many people report to two bosses anyway.

Lack of promotion prospects is a serious disadvantage of part-time jobs; a woman employed on a part-time basis in the Housing Department of a London Borough saw that one of the main advantages of job sharing to her was as a way to promotion on a part-time basis, as she wanted to get on to the career ladder. She has now achieved this, as have two librarians in Sheffield who were working part-time for the City Libraries and were unlikely to be promoted. They teamed up and applied for a senior library assistant job.

After about 6 months they were accepted, and despite 'some suspicion from middle management grades' there is enthusiasm for the way it is working. They themselves feel it has been a positive step since it made them eligible for future promotion, which they achieved in July 1984; they are now the Central Children's Librarian in Sheffield.

In the late 1970s there was a fair amount of information available from the USA on job sharing, since quite a range of jobs were being shared there; however, in the UK there were few examples. A number of the clearing banks had been using alternate week workers for secretarial and administrative posts since the 1940s, although this form of working is not supported by the union, BIFU. Other sharers known of at this time included a pair at the House of Commons Library who started in 1972, and a married couple who began sharing a lectureship at Lancaster University in 1976. Initially they saw sharing as a way of enabling them both to have a job in the same university; 'It's hard enough to get one job when you're an academic, let alone two at the same university'. They have continued with the arrangement since the birth of their child, and now share childcare. The first UK survey of job sharing was carried out by the Equal Opportunities Commission in January 1980, and this looked at the details of twenty-four shared posts, including hospital consultant, planning assistant, librarian and lecturer. All the jobs were in the public and voluntary sector, and three-quarters of the sharers were women. A US survey by Gretl Meier of Stanford University in 1977 found that 60 per cent were in the public sector and educational institutions, and 80 per cent of the sharers were women. Since the EOC survey, the range of shared jobs has widened considerably. There are now many examples in such types of employment as teaching, library work, community work, social work and secretarial work. Other examples include probation officers, GPs, telephonists, lecturers, immigration officers, planners, youth workers, careers officers, caretakers, shop managers, hostel supervisors, solicitors and personnel officers.

Experience in the USA has shown that, although employers may initially be cautious about job sharing, when experiments have proved successful and various advantages have been identified, many are willing to extend its use further. Some of the advantages most frequently quoted by employers are 'the opportunity to retain skilled and experienced staff who may no longer feel able to work full time' and 'the benefit of a wider range of skills and experience'. Another real advantage is that working part-time enables people to stay fresh, energetic and creative during the hours they are working.

A German study published in 1981 by a team from Mannheim University measured the output difference between full-time and job-sharing employees in thirty-five medium sized companies in the Rhineland. The results indicated productivity gains averaging 33 per cent for job sharing. The majority of sharers in the EOC survey believed that employers did get more out of two people doing a job rather than one. Barry Simons, Assistant Borough Housing Officer in Haringey, felt 'job sharers make a very good contribution to the working of any office and because of the fact that they work fewer hours, they are in essence more productive'. He also comments that 'any increase in costs is counterbalanced by the amount of work you get from two part-timers compared to a single employee'. Although there may be some slight additional costs to employers, most feel these are outweighed by the advantages. Rhiannon Chapman, Head of Personnel at the Stock Exchange, feels that 'there is no significant increase in cost involved in having two job sharers'.

Job sharing has attracted considerable debate over the last few years in West Germany. In 1980 the Federation for the Chemical Industry drew up a model job-sharing contract, which allows the hours the sharers do to differ, although they must balance in the long run. The participants are jointly responsible for the whole job, but have separate contracts. A second model agreement was drawn up by the Christian Democrat Party in 1981, but there was criticism of both agreements from the Social Democrats and the DGB trade union confederation. They are concerned about the lack of flexibility for the employee, and the requirement that the partners must be prepared to stand in for one another. This is generally considered to be bad practice in the UK, as an employer already has the advantage of at least half of the job being covered when one sharer is off sick or on holiday. In the UK, although job sharing to a large extent continues to be initiated by individuals, a number of employers have opened up more posts for sharing over the years. One of the earlier schemes has been operated by Lothian Health Board since 1975; initially for doctors in hard to fill areas, the concept has been further developed over the years, and currently includes two consultant posts. Another employer who started with one partnership in 1972 has since expanded the scheme to include twelve posts at junior and senior level; one of these is shared by someone on the verge of retirement. In the voluntary sector International Voluntary Service was another early user of job sharers, and continues to use them. The original pair were a husband and wife team in a field officer post in the Comoro Islands in 1977, who now share a job in South East England. The Inner London Probation Service, with one probation officer post shared since 1981, now has five such shared posts, one of which is shared by someone who after 10 years as a probation officer felt 'burnt out'.

In the USA the most extensive experimentation with job sharing has taken place within the public sector. Efforts to implement alternative work patterns began in the mid-1970s, when a number of states initiated demonstration projects, the number of employees involved ranging from 50 to 2,000. Government, particularly at the local state level, has played an important part in initiating and encouraging alternative work patterns. By 1982 twenty-five states and the federal government had officially encouraged the use of job sharing and other forms of permanent part time employment by passing legislation that specifically increased the opportunities for such work arrangements, or by supporting pilot projects designed to test the feasibility of allowing employees to reduce the number of hours in their current jobs.

Similarly the most exciting recent developments of job-sharing schemes in the UK have taken place in the public sector, and a number of local authorities now have job-sharing policies at various stages of development. The London Borough of Hackney was one of the first to announce a policy in December 1981. Initially this was very slow to be implemented, and at this time the Hackney Job Share Project saw the main problem as 'the need to inform both management and employees as to the benefits of job sharing and how it should be put into practice'. Over the last two years the Project has worked closely with the Training and Personnel Departments of Hackney Council; this has included running training sessions for managers and supervisors.

The hard work is now beginning to pay off, since the policy now opens up all posts within the Council to job sharers – advertisements state that 'job shared applications will be welcomed with or without a partner'. Should a manager consider that a post is not suitable for sharing, it has to be specifically exempted and approved by the director of that department. All exempted posts are being monitored and reported regularly to the Equal Opportunities Sub-Committee. All council employees have been informed of their right to job share via a leaflet in the pay packet, and information has appeared with internal job advertisements. In addition, a register has been set up to help people find partners. The success or failure of the policy is being monitored by the Personnel Department, which is following up all job-sharing applications. In March 1984 there were twenty posts within Hackney being shared: these include two librarians, a personnel assistant, telephonist and three area social workers.

A number of other local authorities now have policies in varying stages of development; these include the London Borough of Camden, with thirty shared posts; Lewisham; the Greater London Council; West Midlands; Glasgow; and Sheffield. Compared with only 3 years ago, the number of advertisements for jobs in the public sector which state that they are open to job-share applicants have increased greatly. To what extent such policies are taken seriously is another question; there is at least a chance in areas where job-sharing applicants are monitored (as they are in Hackney) and where positive training is given to managers.

Where a particular department has employed sharers and found the experience a success, it is then usually more willing to employ others. In Sheffield the policy is most developed in the Social Services Department where fourteen posts are currently shared. These include social workers, community workers, typists, a nursery officer and a district home-help organiser. Of the four social work posts, one is at a senior principal level. When asked what it considered to be the advantages for employers, the Social Services Department highlighted greater flexibility, retention of skilled and experienced employees, and help towards equality for women.

For workers in local authorities a serious problem remains with respect to the Local Government Superannuation Scheme, which currently excludes people working less than 30 hours a week unless they have been in the scheme continuously with the same employer since 1 April 1974. Draft regulations to amend these to include those who work for 15 hours or more have been under consideration by the government for at least 3 years. In the UK central government has been slow to introduce the job-sharing option for its own employees. The Department of Health and Social Security is the first government department to have reached an agreement with a civil service trade union on a comprehensive and accountable system for the introduction of job sharing, and this is to be carefully monitored.

The number of job sharers in the voluntary sector has grown considerably in recent years, and in March 1983 a conference on job sharing and voluntary organisations was sponsored jointly by the National Council for Voluntary Organisations and New Ways to Work. Many voluntary organisations are now opening their jobs to job-sharing applicants. A particular advantage in a small organisation with only one full-time post is that sharing can help break down isolation, as well as providing someone else to talk through ideas and share responsibility with.

In the USA job-sharing arrangements in the private sector have tended to be the outcome of individual negotiations. However, interest has grown and there are teams of job sharers employed by several large companies, including Control Data, Hewlett-Packard and Levis. In the UK again there are a number of individuals in the private sector who have negotiated shares, but the main examples in private companies have come about primarily as a response to youth unemployment. A scheme introduced by GEC Telecommunications at its Coventry plant in June 1981 was for school leavers. Following its success GEC introduced a scheme at its Newton Aycliffe plant. Here the option was given to existing employees and to workers who had been made redundant earlier in the year. This scheme has received the support of the three unions concerned. Although advocates of these schemes feel that job sharing can play an important role in easing unemployment, critics feel that, as with the government's job-splitting scheme, part-time jobs are being offered to those who really want and need full-time work. Young people, on low wages, are one group least likely to want job sharing as a positive choice.

In the USA there has been a national Job Sharing Network since 1979. In 1983 it changed its name to the National Network for Work Time Options, reflecting its interest in other work time alternatives. A 2-year project is currently under way to develop and exchange information about alternative work time, using microcomputers. In the UK New Ways to Work (formerly the Job Share Project) has been the main organisation promoting job sharing since 1977. It is national in outlook, but is at present financed for work within the Greater London area only. It provides advice for individuals, employers and trade unions, and has a range of publications on job sharing, in addition to the job-sharing partner service already referred to. It is the central clearing house for information on job sharing in the UK. Another group in London is the Hackney Job Share Project, which operates within the London Borough of Hackney, and has produced an exhibition and two videos on job sharing.

Over the last few years a number of local groups have set up around the country; these include Lewisham and Southwark, Sheffield and Bristol. An enthusiastic group of people in Scotland organised a conference in Glasgow in November 1982 which was attended by about 100 individuals, including trade union representatives and employers.

Unfortunately attempts to finance the group have so far been unsuccessful, as have efforts to obtain funds for other local groups. Leicester is one exception, where, following a conference on job sharing held in December 1982, the local Council for Voluntary Service sponsored a project for two years exploring the possibilities for job sharing locally. This has now obtained two secondees from local industry, who are sharing the equivalent of a full-time job between them. New Ways to Work itself continues to seek finance for its national work. So far it has not received any statutory funding from central government, one of the problems being that the ideas it is promoting do not fit comfortably into the responsibilities of any one government department.

Teaching is an area where there has been a great interest in job sharing. Although part-time teaching posts have been available, they are invariably on the lowest scale and are of low status within the school. In the USA teaching was one of the first job areas in which job sharing proved to be successful. A survey carried out in 1982 by New Ways to Work; San Francisco, found that, out of California's 1,041 school districts, 387 had implemented job-sharing programmes for teachers – that amounted to 1500 teachers in California working under this option. In the UK there has also been a large amount of interest in job sharing among teachers, but here its use has developed more slowly. A scheme was introduced by Sheffield Education Authority in 1981, and by September 1983 twenty teaching posts were being shared. Initially the local union, the National Union of Teachers (NUT), was rather antagonistic, but it has now drawn up notes of guidance, as has the NUT nationally.

One of the most contentious issues has been whether job sharers should be able to hold posts above scale 1, as this is seen by some as taking promotion prospects away from full-timers. Currently in Sheffield most are scale 1 posts, but there are a few at scale 2 and 3. In the USA some head teachers share posts, one of these being the job of principal of a centre of 950 students (aged 9–14) in Washington DC. They share all the responsibilities, including the supervision of eighteen teachers, and have not had any major problems as a result of their job sharing.

A study of sharing arrangements in ten Sheffield schools, published late in 1984, indicated that the advantages to heads included the children having 'gained from watching two people working and co-operating together'. The two sharers also benefited from having to talk about their work to each other, because they had been forced to think more about their approach to teaching.

In April 1984 the Inner London Education Authority (ILEA) approved a pilot scheme for thirty teaching posts to be shared for an initial period of 12 months, following a successful pilot job share of a scale 2 post since 1982. The scheme is being rushed through despite lack of union support with a view to its being effective from September 1984. The Inner London Teachers Association (ILTA), who have taken part in negotiations with the ILEA, are generally in favour of the introduction of job sharing, but oppose the present scheme on two grounds. Firstly, it will not apply to all posts, as headships and deputy headships will be excluded, as will pastoral heads also, unless the head teacher, inspector and chair of governors all agree otherwise. Secondly, the scheme makes no provision for the payment of overlap time. The ILTA sought for the payment of half a day each week for sharers at scale 1, which would have meant a total extra cost of approximately £30,000. The members of the ILEA sub-committee, however, rejected overlap time as unnecessary, although they agreed to monitor the scheme to see if problems did arise.

There is now a job-sharing support group for teachers in Greater London, and within this there has been much discussion centred on the ILEA scheme, which also gives teachers the opportunity to exchange ideas. The group is to continue to press for overlap time to be recognised during the pilot scheme.

Trade union responses to the issue of job sharing in the UK have been variable. Initially there was very little attention paid to the idea. Unions have traditionally not had much to do with part-timers, owing to the difficulties of organising them, and fears that part-timers might be used to undercut full-time rates of pay.

Because of the development of job-sharing schemes in a

number of local authorities, the National and Local Government Officers Association (NALGO) has been one union which has been most active in its promotion as an equal opportunities measure. Sheffield City Council NALGO took part in very detailed negotiations in drawing up a job-sharing agreement with the Council. Nationally NALGO does not have a policy on the subject, although it broadly supports job sharing and in its booklet on Rights of Working Parents (*A Negotiating Kit*, published in September 1981) it recognises job sharing as 'an exciting development in part time work'. The 1981 NALGO membership survey of 5,000 members (half men, half women) on equality attempted to test the latent demand for job sharing, and found that 1 in 20 of male full-timers said that they would prefer to be job sharing rather than working full-time, as did 1 in 10 of the full-time women workers.

Another union with no national policy on job sharing is the NUT, although very detailed notes of guidance have been produced for individual members. The National Association of Probation Officers (NAPO) had a resolution passed at its national conference in 1981 which called for job sharing to be pursued locally by branches, and this has already been happening in London, Leicester and Sheffield. The Civil and Public Services Association (CPSA) is basically in favour of job sharing and has played a part in drawing up an agreement with the Department of Health and Social Security.

In their publication on collective bargaining agreements, *Assistance for Working Parents,* the Trades Union Congress (TUC) recognised the use of job sharing, and stressed that 'unions should make every effort to become involved, at an early stage . . . to ensure that it is a voluntary agreement and that participants do not lose their employment rights and get "pro rata" pay and conditions'. Draft guidelines on job sharing have been prepared by the Women's Advisory Committee of the TUC. These are shortly to be circulated to all TUC affiliated unions in order to collect their views. Although the TUC, NALGO and many other unions came out very strongly against the job-splitting scheme, and although it is clearly not being taken up, it has caused confusion among many.

There is still antagonism towards job sharing in the trade union movement, but as Lil Stevens, President of the National Union of Public Employees (NUPE), said in an article in May 1984, 'There is no contradiction in trade unions taking up the issue of job sharing and ensuring that employees' rights are safeguarded, while recognising that it is not the answer to the problems of the vast majority of women seeking employment or better conditions. It is one more element in opening up the range of opportunities, particularly for women, which the trade unions should not turn their backs on'.

Not only are some unions negotiating job sharing for their members, one union, the National Union of Journalists (NUJ) has agreed job sharing for elected posts within the union. On its 1984 National Executive Committee it has four people sharing two newly created seats.

In the USA, again, unions in general have been slow to embrace job sharing. Teachers and other public sector unions led on the issue, and hundreds of local branches of the teachers' unions have negotiated contracts, as have many public sector unions. In a survey of local union officials in the San Francisco Bay area, 70 per cent of the respondents agreed that 'job sharing can be an organising issue for unions, particularly those organising women and older workers'. Union agreements covering job sharers in the private sector are still rare; much more common are agreements between individual employees and their employers.

A fear expressed by some employers about job sharing is that once people are given the option, everyone will want to do it. However, this is not likely to be the case, as it is doubtful if large numbers will be able to afford to work fewer hours in this way. During the period 1975–78 employees of the City of Palo Alto in California were encouraged to consider job sharing, and by March 1978 1 per cent of the City's workforce were sharing a job. Of 28,000 employees surveyed in another project in the USA, 6 per cent said that at some point in their career they would like to try job sharing. Although it may be a permanent way of working for some people, job sharing for most will be a transitional arrangement. To allow for this, agreements drawn up in some local authorities allow sharers the option of returning to full time when a full-time post at a suitable level becomes available.

Job sharing is not a panacea for the unemployment problem. There will always be people who want to work full-time, and they should not be forced to job share. It is, however, important for those who choose to do so to be able to. Over the years individuals who have started to negotiate job sharing have done so because they have seen it as an opportunity to change their own lives, many of them seeking a balance in the relation between their personal and work needs. In particular, by giving both men and women the opportunity to work part-time, job sharing can challenge the divide between men's work and women's work, and allow them to divide childcare, domestic and paid work between them.

By demonstrating that two people can successfully share a job normally done by one, job sharing can provide an alternative to entrenched ideas that a job means 40 hours a week, and can prove to management that new innovative work patterns are feasible. After all, at the turn of the century the full-time norm was 60 hours a week, so we are all working part time compared with then.

11 Telecommuting

Control Data Corporation (USA)

The reign of the microcomputer will affect the location of work in the future. With the increase in the numbers of employees working at home with a company computer, the fate of the traditional business office is called into question.

As the technologies of data processing and communications advance, an increasingly prevalent side effect is a change in the geography of work. Microcomputers, in particular, have made possible the dispersal of work and the inception of remote, electronic cottages. Labour is already shifting from the office and factory to the home at a rate sufficient to cause predictions of a telecommuting workforce of nearly 10 million in the USA alone by 1990.

Most of these will be 'knowledge' workers, engaged in the organisation and application of information as opposed to the mechanics of production and manufacturing. Linked to a central computer and communications facility, they will perform functions ranging from data processing and computer programming to teaching, engineering, design and strategic planning. Any task whose end product is data (created, manipulated, transferred or informative) can be, and in a matter of time almost certainly will be, performed at a remote workstation.

Factors in support of alternative worksites include the energy savings of employees who no longer need to commute physically; reductions in corporate overheads for space and administrative facilities; and the steadily declining cost of the technologies necessary for telecommuting.

In the case of Control Data Corporation, however, the

initial impetus for an alternative worksite programme arose
from a wholly different perspective: the desire to recapture
the productive abilities of company employees who became
disabled. In 1978, Control Data, a US-based computer and
financial services multinational, instituted a programme to
retrain disabled employees to do computer-based work at
their homes, and the success of this venture (called
Homework) led the company to examine the issues of
alternative worksites in more detail.

Control Data makes and sells some of the world's largest
and most powerful computers, along with a full line of
computer peripherals. It offers computer services such as
timesharing, data processing, audience measurement, and
educational and consulting programs, and through the
Commercial Credit Company subsidiary markets consumer
and business financial services. Control Data has nearly
60,000 employees in forty-seven countries, and annual
revenues of approximately $4.5 billion.

Over the past 15 years the company's business strategy has
been to address society's major unfulfilled needs as profitable business opportunities. Instead of making products and
then trying to create a desire for them, Control Data has
tried to identify needs that already exist, and then to tailor
business solutions to those needs.

Clearly, there is no shortage of things an international
society needs, from more affordable health care to more
available quality education, and the company has committed
itself to these and other non-traditional markets. In almost
every case the eventual product of service began as an
internal project – Staywell, for example, a health maintenance program, and Plato computer-based education were
both developed and refined extensively through internal
Control Data use before being offered to customers. In
effect, the company population is large enough to serve as a
test market.

Homework arose from the realisation that Control Data,
like every other large company, was suffering enormous
losses, both in money and expertise, whenever one of its
trained workers became disabled. Across the US there are
currently more than 2 million people homebound through

handicap, illness, and social dependence, most of whom were at one time productive, accomplished workers. But where they once contributed to the economy, now they cost US taxpayers more than $750 million each month in social security payments alone.

To the individual company, the loss of an employee results not only in direct costs of unemployment compensation and insurance payments, but in the much greater indirect costs of training a replacement and writing off accumulated expertise. At a technology-based company the talents and knowledge of many long-term employees can be impossible to replicate at any price. For the disabled employee, beyond the obvious physical concerns, there are the very painful problems of loneliness, loss of self-esteem, and monotony.

Control Data chose to view disabled workers not as incapable of work, but as simply unable to *get* to work in the traditional sense. The question then became, how could work be taken to them? The answer was in retraining and equipping them to work at home. Central to this was the use of PLATO computer-based education.

PLATO is an educational system that makes use of a range of courseware stored in a central computer or on floppy disks. Materials are displayed on the screen in the form of numbers, text, drawings, and animated graphics. The screen, keyboard, and other equipment can come in the form of a terminal tied to a central computer, or a stand-alone microprocessor. Individual courses can also direct a user to a variety of other media – tapes, slides, books, and so on.

As an instruction device, PLATO displays infinite patience and personalisation. It can diagnose a student's needs, teach, drill, test, and do it in an individualised, self-paced manner. The user progresses only as quickly as he or she can master the material. PLATO also offers the ability to update, flashback, review, explain, and animate. It can simulate nearly any activity, such as the operation of aircraft navigation systems. Currently, there are more than 1,200 titles and 10,000 hours of PLATO courseware available, with courses ranging from basic grammar through to high school maths, to advanced business and technical instruction.

There is also the potential for modifications to PLATO, which made it physically accessible to people with a variety of disabilities. Another feature significant to Homework participants is the ability of PLATO users to communicate with one another via their computer terminals. As a result, a communications network developed among them which fulfilled many of the social functions that office conversations provide in a normal business setting.

The first PLATO terminal was installed in August 1978 in the home of one of the first twelve Homework volunteers chosen. The initial work selected for Homeworkers to perform was to design and evaluate educational courseware for the system itself. Depending on their interest, experience and skill, each participant was then trained to perform one of these three functions via the PLATO terminal. The end product of Homework thus became educational courseware marketed for profit by Control Data and delivered on Plato.

Control Data expanded homebound employment the next year, making additions to the types of work performed to include computer programming, remote student tutoring and other functions. From this early experience certain benefits began to accrue. Health care costs for the Homework participants, for example, decreased by 50 to 75 per cent. After starting the program, some Homeworkers found that regular visits to their doctors were no longer necessary. Among the group as a whole, self-concept and confidence levels increased substantially, improvements in family relations occurred, higher levels of self-care were realised, and enhanced intellectual and cognitive functioning was apparent. These preliminary findings parallel the results from a 7-year study on homebound rehabilitation sponsored by the Federation of the Handicapped and funded by the US Department of Health, Education and Welfare.

The success of Homework in its first two years led Control Data to examine the larger issues of alternative worksites, and to start a more far-reaching programme in its Professional Services division. This group, composed of engineers, systems analysts, programmers, management consultants and educators, spent the next two years in alternative worksites.

In general, Control Data's workforce mirrors the emerging employee population worldwide: that is, it is increasingly diverse in terms of age, race, sex, education, background and ability. Among other things, the US workforce is getting older, and minority workers are increasingly filling entry-level positions. It is understood that an effective manager must be a good communicator in order to reach and motivate in this environment, and he or she must be oriented toward people rather than solely toward production. Thinking must be holistic rather than linear, both in regard to projects and to people.

In the information age, the business of Control Data and other similar companies is the gathering and distribution of knowledge, a uniquely human product. Employees become a critical and uncertain link in the process, and their management becomes crucial. Workers are no longer motivated solely by financial gain. Nor is their loyalty given solely to their company; it often focuses on their profession. People are more apt to think of a career not as long-term employment with one company, but as a progression of challenges and advancements in a particular field and, if need be, through several companies. The cost of training replacements is expensive, both in time and productivity.

It was against this background that Control Data began its alternative worksite programme, under which selected employees began to work either from home or from small satellite offices near their homes. Initially, the form of work led to problems in productivity and quality control. How does one measure and assign work to be done out of sight? It turned out that the amount of work completed was as important to the employee as it was to the company. 'How am I doing in relation to others?' was a common, if unstated, question – one that does not arise when the 'others' are just across the hall.

To deal with the issue, Control Data limited the type of work done to those things with a definite beginning, middle, and end. Employees worked on a project basis, with defined milestones and a specific result or product to be delivered at a specific time. This meant reliance had to be placed on managers to be sensitive to employee needs for support, recognition and structure. It fell to managers to keep employees challenged, and at the same time to respond to their individual needs. This required, among other things, the ability to create an environment of caring, to communicate openly a concern for employees.

The role of telecommuter manager, rather than that of sitting at an apex, is one of strategic planning and consensus-gathering, both of which put a premium on communicating effectively. In addition, it was discovered that there is an even greater need for structure in this style of work and management than in more traditional styles. People want to know what they are expected to do, and the manager must be able to communicate expectations of service and output effectively. One technique that evolved was a form of contract between manager and employee for specific products or services within a set time. The company also adopted a more formal project tracking system, an automated process for monitoring control, the implementation of which became the responsibility of the manager. In the end a telecommuting strategy must include definitions of productivity that are clear and satisfactory to the employee, the manager, and to corporate management.

After one year of the alternative worksite programme, Control Data found that the productivity of the participating workers had improved. Two major reasons were identified: first, with little or no time required in going to and from work, employees had more time to spend working; second, because working at or near one's home was desirable to many, their motivation was higher. In addition, because they were free of the stresses inherent in commuting, participants reported feeling more refreshed when they started work. They also had fewer distractions and were able to work faster and with greater concentration. Accordingly, workers noted productivity increases ranging from 12 to 20 per cent.

Of course, human beings are social animals, and not everyone adapts well to the potentially lonely working environment of the electronic cottage. The fear of isolation is a real one, as is the fear of dehumanisation by machines. These must be countered through civilising influences and a sense of community among workers, the sort of social interplay provided daily in the old office by a joke in the hall or lunch with a friend. At Control Data this human need produced an interesting phenomenon: underground computer-based gossip. This electronic answer to the coffee break is a regular computer-stored series of conversations, jokes, games, non-sequiturs and running commentary. It can be called up at any time anywhere in the world, and it instantly puts an employee in touch with his or her peers.

Despite a willingness – and in many cases a desire – to work alone, telecommuting employees still evidenced a need to belong. Therefore, it was essential that those who worked at home were included in meetings and regular functions with other employees.

Control Data managers held mandatory meetings at least once each month with their remote employees. Many of these workers had both an alternative worksite and a central office station, though the majority of their work was completed at the alternative site, be it in their homes or in a satellite office.

Along with certain characteristics required in a manager of remote employees, so too the successful telecommuting employee has certain attributes. He or she is highly motivated to succeed, tends to be more mature than in-house employees, is a self-starter, and does not need constant supervision. Some of the initial Control Data volunteers thought they fitted this profile, but after several months found themselves becoming lax. They realised they needed the proximity of co-workers and the stimulus of an office environment in order to produce.

Employees can also fall prey to the feeling that out of sight is out of mind, a fear that if they are not seen they will not be appreciated and that promotions might suffer as a result. Constant encouragement and regular productivity reviews by management are required to mitigate these concerns.

The question of company loyalty also arises in the context of telecommuting employees. In the Control Data experience, however, this was not a problem – perhaps because the workers saw themselves as pioneers, and saw Control Data as a company sensitive to their needs. Moreover, participants could claim some attractive benefits as a result. For example, some cut their driving by 500 miles per month – a saving of up to $100 in transportation costs alone. In California car insurance costs have been lowered by as much as 30 per cent. Participants also saved on food and clothing (although one participant who used to bring his lunch to work and read during the noon hour now found he needed to leave home at lunch time in order to re-establish human contact – thereby spending more on food.)

The very fact that some alternative worksite employees benefit financially poses a problem. The issue is that of 'compensating benefits' for traditional employees who must still commute to work and arrange for meals away from home. Similar administrative problems arise in the areas of tax and insurance, and as yet there are no concrete answers.

At a conceptual level the electronic cottage holds the potential for both achievement and abuse. To the homebound – the disabled, or those with children to look after – it may represent their only access to a meaningful job. To other workers it offers the entrepreneurial ideal of independence, a liberating style of work that eliminates the routine of set hours and settled pay. To a corporation the benefits can include greater productivity, lower costs in overhead and administration, and access to an untapped labour pool. On the other hand, organised labour fears a return to the piecework sweatshops of the late nineteenth century, with the computer terminal standing in for the sewing machine. The unions imagine companies cutting back office staff and parcelling work out to low-paid clerical workers at home. Essentially unable to organise and to bargain for higher wages, these pieceworkers might try to supplement their earnings by putting other family members – including children – to work. This version of a domestic electronic sweatshop, however, has yet to appear in fact.

In practical terms, it is Control Data's experience that the success of a telecommuting program on a large scale depends on the manager–employee relation. Interestingly, the greatest obstacles tend to come from managers rather than employees. Those schooled in production tend to believe, 'You can't trust people you can't see'. Unable to walk out from their offices and look over their staff, some managers experience 'loss of stage', or fear of losing control. Because ego can play a large part in management, some managers equate a loss of visible employees with a loss of power.

The answer to these and similar problems is education. Managers can be made to understand that their responsibilities will be enhanced under a system of remote workers. In the short term they will be seen as pioneers, and given increased attention within the company. Over the long term they will be able to supervise more people more efficiently. Use of electronic communications will enable them to reach more workers more frequently than is possible in person and with less chance of strategic misunderstandings. Further, if there is a problem in the system, it will come to light quickly.

Another source of manager resistance stems from 'keyboard fever', the fear of electronic technology. As with any fear of change, this too is solved through education. As one learns more about the use and potential of computers, for example, fear of the unknown inevitably dissolves into a fascination with the possibilities.

Managers will come to realise the benefits of telecommunications. They can be used, for example, in an alternative worksite setting as ways to reach group consensus, as mediators, as tools for performing tasks better suited to computers than employees, and for pulling together and analysing data. Managers will learn to manage a process rather than just people, although the traditional managerial attributes of intuition and good judgement will always play a role. Managers will become increasingly computer-literate, and will be better able to understand and access the ever-increasing volume of knowledge stored electronically. Managers will have to learn how to supervise workers who are becoming more and more specialised: as these specialisations develop, the tasks of training, retraining and integrating employees into the productive structure will become more difficult and time-consuming.

The company that cannot effectively and inexpensively train its new employees, and train replacements for its skilled workers, cannot compete. For both traditional employees and remote workers, the logical answer is computer-based education and training. It offers a vehicle for delivering both general and highly specialised courseware and instruction across a broad spectrum of need, from basic literacy skills to state-of-the-art technical advancements.

Computer-based education is perhaps the only mechanism able to store, transmit, and deliver individualised instruction on the scale and with the speed necessary to meet the current and projected needs of business. Moreover, it can be made flexible and sensitive enough to accommodate individuals of widely varying backgrounds and abilities, and can be delivered on demand, on-site, wherever an individual chooses to work.

It is estimated that 250 US companies have some form of work at home programme, with roughly 10,000 telecommuting employees, and that an equal number of people work independently out of electronic cottages. With the rapid advances in microcomputer technology and applications, those numbers can be expected to swell. If, as forecast, 80 per cent of business people end up with personal computers on their desks, more and more of those desks will be outside the traditional business office.

DATE DUE